RURAL ODYSSEY:
Growing Up in the Country

RURAL ODYSSEY
Growing Up in the Country

Memories of Family, Faith, and Secrets

Dr. RL Carroll

ELM HILL

A Division of
HarperCollins Christian Publishing

www.elmhillbooks.com

RURAL ODYSSEY:
Growing Up in the Country
Memories of Family, Faith, and Secrets

Published in Nashville, Tennessee, by Elm Hill, an imprint of Thomas Nelson. Elm Hill and Thomas Nelson are registered trademarks of HarperCollins Christian Publishing, Inc.

Elm Hill titles may be purchased in bulk for educational, business, fund-raising, or sales promotional use. For information, please e-mail SpecialMarkets@Thomas Nelson.com.

Library of Congress Cataloging-in-Publication Data

Library of Congress Control Number: 2018940973

ISBN 978-1-595556684 (Paperback)
ISBN 978-1-595556103 (Hardbound)
ISBN 978-1-595557070 (eBook)

PROLOGUE

I do not believe in coincidences. In fact in the Hebrew language there is no word for coincidence. God opens and closes doors in our lives. So if there is a choice between miracle and coincidence, miracle wins out every time. Not until I read *Hillbilly Elegy*, a memoir of a family and culture in crisis by J.D Vance, did I realize I had a similar but different story.

One definition of *stupidity* is *doing the same thing over and over and expecting different results*. If you don't know your family history and you don't learn from it, you're destined to repeat it. In essence this is my family history and my history of growing up in the country. No one has ever known most of it or taken the time to record it. This is my story and I hope by relating it, some can learn from or avoid certain things that have happened to me. My family history and story are in many ways similar to Mr. Vance's story. The main differences lie in two categories. One of them is the secrets that were kept by my family and most other families I grew up with. The second is that basic Pentecostal fundamentalist religious beliefs were present.

My story commences with growing up in South Carolina for my first ten years before moving to Tennessee where I lived for fifty-four years (except for two years spent in the Army at Redstone Arsenal in Huntsville, Alabama). Then I moved to rural Florida where I have lived and worked for the past eleven years. Even though the states changed and I grew older, the stories remained the same, as do the secrets and my religious faith. I have spent the past forty-one years as a board-certified general surgeon with almost all of the time being spent in rural America. I'm now seventy-five years old and have had a very full and eventful life. These are my memories and may not be correct in all details, but it is how I remember them. My faith remains strong, though it has wavered many times throughout my life as it has with others. This is highlighted in many of the memories I have and in the people that surrounded me.

Looking back, most of the regions I grew up in had no people of color. I did not consider this to be an advantage or hindrance as much as a mere fact of growing up. Others may disagree, but I do not feel this made a difference in the way I was raised or in my relationship to people throughout my entire life. Even after we have moved to Florida, I found we were still in the country. In fact, if you cut the crust off the state of Florida, there is nothing left but country. I now live in an area that is best described as being 50 percent Hispanic, many of whom are illegal, and most speak very little English. Approximately 25 percent of the population are African-American (I grew up calling them *blacks*), and the other 25 percent are white like me.

Two things have been consistent in my life and I also believe in rural America—faith and secrets. My definition of *faith* is taken from Hebrews 11: 1 which states, "Now faith is the substance of things hoped for, the evidence of things not seen." A *secret* is defined as something kept from the knowledge of others or shared only confidentially with a few. I was always warned that telling secrets was taboo. *I'm going to tell a lot of them.* I guess they will remain a secret to those don't read the book. I have always been careful when I picked friends, and I don't think it will make any difference to most of them. I have one friend who says, "If you can't see it until you see it, you'll never see it." I wholeheartedly agree. I think this is true of both faith and secrets.

I came up with a brilliant bibliography for my facts- none. I learned how to reference material when I began writing reports and papers in high school. I was told in my residency that I needed to be published. It was understood that my work must have a bibliography. But I also learned that I can come up with articles to prove the exact opposite of what the facts really are. You can come up with your own bibliography to prove your own facts. I have mine. One study shows that less than 2 percent of readers ever look at bibliographies, 10–15 percent know in general what bibliographies are, and the other 80–85 percent wonder what the little numbers represent.

Peter, my youngest son who recently passed away, used to say, "Daddy, tell me a story about when you were a little boy." At the encouragement of my family, my students, and my friends, I decided to tell the stories. Dale Gentry, a prophetic minister and a friend, gave me the following words: "I have set you like a lily in the midst of a valley. There is an attraction about your life that people are drawn to. In the midst of what looks like a desolate situation, you are always going to become like the lily that shines forth. I have made your tongue like the pen of a ready writer … there are times when you say words and it comes like a story in people's lives and gives them hope. There is a book inside of you. If you will speak the book, it will be written…. **You must tell the stories** and people's faith in life will get hope. You are at the right time and place for a **Holy Ghost** invasion."

Here are the stories…

CHAPTER 1

My father's family came from the northern portion of the state of Georgia. My dad's father was Amer Jackson Carroll and his identical twin brother was Amos Johnson Carroll. According to oral history, both men were considered to be wealthy and owned the entire upper half of the state of Georgia (an exaggeration I'm sure) until they started drinking whiskey. They eventually became alcoholics and "lost it all," wealth and land.

My grandfather Amer and his wife Bertie Belle Cochran along with their children moved from Franklin County, Georgia, to Greenville, South Carolina. At an earlier time, his brother Amos had moved to Greenville to find work in the "cotton mill" there. The identical twins actually lived around the corner from each other in Dunean, the "mill town" surrounding the J. P. Stevens Dunean Textile Plant in Greenville. Amos had found work there in the cotton or textile mill for himself and for most of the members of his and his brother's family. Even when the children grew up and married, they usually lived within a few blocks of each other. All the houses in the mill village were architecturally laid out the same. I heard many stories about fights at work and at home in this close-knit area. They were usually alcohol-related. At home everyone could tell what room the disputes were in because of the sameness and closeness of the houses.

My grandfather and grandmother had seven children. The oldest was Aunt Joy who lived to be ninety-five. Uncle Robert was a Baptist deacon who died of a heart attack in his early sixties. When he married Myra, they moved to a house two blocks away from where the family lived when they moved to Greenville. They had three daughters. I attended Uncle Robert's funeral at Dunean Baptist Church in 1970. The only thing I remember at the service was that the minister said Uncle Robert was a "good man." Next was Uncle J. B. (only the initials), who eventually legally named himself John Benjamin. He married "Boots" and they had no children. He lived to be eighty-seven. Uncle Quinton became a Baptist minister and passed away at fifty-six from a stroke. He and his wife had four daughters. Aunt Rama, who is now over one hundred years of age, married a Church of God minister and had a daughter and son. Aunt Lucille and her husband were lifelong Church of God members and had two daughters. The baby and seventh child of the family was my father who was born in 1920 and had one son, me.

My father started his adult life working in the mill. Part of his job included tying knots from the end of the cotton thread coming off one bobbin to the beginning thread of the next bobbin. He told me he could do this very quickly using either his right or left hand. I now tie knots in surgery with either hand except I use silk, Prolene, or biologically absorbable sutures (cotton sutures were being phased out when I started my surgical training). At age twenty, he was considered managerial material for the textile mill and was offered a raise in pay. Mother and Dad had serious conversations about his being called to the ministry and leaving the textile mill where he had financial security. This caused them a lot of frustration initially but then both agreed that Dad would become a minister. Mother had her nineteenth birthday on February 7, 1942, and "secretly" eloped with Dad who was twenty-one years old. They were married on February 14, 1942. They came home to Greenville and lived separately with other family members. Mother's sister Odine had moved to Greenville from Louisiana to live and work with a family friend who was a minister. Dad and mother realized they needed to make everyone aware of their secret marriage because of the possibility that Mother would become pregnant. They let everyone know and sure enough, I was born ten months later on December 27, 1942. I've always said I was almost a "Christmas Carroll." Years later after I became a doctor, I asked my mother if she had had a period before I was born. She was embarrassed and replied, "Only you would ask," and admitted that she had had one period after she and Dad were married.

Dad had preached his first sermon in Greenville, South Carolina, at the Tremont Avenue Church of God, when he was eighteen years old. He preached his last sermon at the same church on January 26, 1972. He died at fifty-one years old, the same age his mother was when she passed away. Several weeks before he went to Greenville that last time, Dad had asked me to bring home all the necessary materials to do a rectal exam. Along with hypertension and adult onset diabetes (both secret and untreated), he was having problems with rectal bleeding. The exam, done in the bedroom of my house in Chattanooga, confirmed the fact that Dad had a carcinoma of the rectum. An appointment was set up for him to see a colorectal surgeon the week after he returned from Greenville. Another "secret" never mentioned until now.

All my life I loved to hear stories about our family. Almost all of my grandfather Amer and grandmother Bertie's early history has been lost because Dad and all his brothers and sisters could not or would not tell me anything about him. The only early story I remember about my grandfather I heard my father use in sermons as an example of God's protection. The incident occurred when Amer took his wife Bertie and four kids to town in Georgia to get groceries.

While they were inside the general store, Amer went to a bar and got drunk. When he finally returned, his family had been waiting in the horse-drawn buggy. During the drive home, he promised to use the horse whip and teach his wife a lesson. Who knows what the reason for the lesson was except his drunkenness. Everyone was scared. All Bertie knew to do was pray. As they were nearing home and the buggy wheels hit the wooden bridge over a small creek, it seemed that divine intervention caused Amer to fall asleep. When they arrived home he awakened in a drunken rage. Again all Bertie knew to do was pray. Amer took the whip and struck at his wife multiple times. All the whippings were turned away by surrounding angels and not one of the lashes hit her. When he was tired of the physical exercise, he was led inside the house and went to sleep. Coincidence of being drunk or miracle?

The second story about my grandfather came years later at a family reunion at a cousin's home in Greenwood, South Carolina. Most of the family and cousins were present—my father had passed away a couple of years earlier. I asked Joy, the oldest of the brothers and sisters, what happened to my grandfather Amer. She was very hesitant to begin a conversation. I told her that Dad would never say anything and I thought I had a right to know our family history. She begrudgingly told this story.

Amer brought his wife and children to Greenville, South Carolina. Aunt Joy was sixteen years old at the time they moved. My grandfather had also brought a sixteen-year-old girl who was his mistress. They all lived in the same house at 211 Allen Street in Dunean, the mill village. Evidently Amer, who was forty-five years old at the time, and his sixteen-year-old mistress got in an argument. At some point in the argument and fight that ensued, she picked up a handgun that was lying on the dresser, shot him, and calmly laid the gun down. He, in a fit of rage, picked up the gun and shot her. It must have been a small caliber gun or Amer and his young mistress were very poor shots, because both died slowly over the next several days. Of course nothing was ever done about the crime and I'm not sure it was ever reported. My grandmother Bertie did not remarry and reared her seven children until her baby, my dad, was eighteen years old. She passed away in March 1940 with uterine cancer about two and a half years before I was born.

As Joy was telling this story of what had happened, the entire family gathered around her. Each wanted to give their recollections. Joy promptly stopped them and said she was actually present and remembered exactly what happened. No matter, I had finally exposed a family secret—one of many secrets that were kept and passed down through my family until this day.

My mother, dad, and I spent several weekends over several years while I was growing up looking for my grandfather's grave around many of the small cemeteries and churches in Franklin County, Georgia. Using all the information we could get from family, friends, and neighbors, we looked for a white unmarked flint or granite headstone supposedly located under a flowering white bush but never found his grave site.

Dad told me many times that all our family were either alcoholics or ministers. This began my pilgrimage of secrets and faith, major aspects of my life. However, the cost of secrets can be generational. In the book *Before We Were Yours* by Lisa Wingate, one of her characters stated "Secrets have a way of coming out," and "Secrets also make you vulnerable to your enemies." (p. 162)

Aunt Joy had married Carl and they had three children—two girls and a boy. Carl was an alcoholic who rode a motorcycle, a dangerous combination. One evening while drunk, he stood on the seat of his motorcycle and rode at a dangerous speed onto a bridge. The expansion joint at the start of the bridge caused him to be pitched from the bike, landing on his head with the expected results. Joy never remarried and her children grew up with no father. Once when visiting with family in Greenville, I was invited to play underneath one of the old houses in the neighborhood. The porch was about five feet above the ground. The teenage boy who invited me to play underneath the house was an acquaintance of the family and while we were there, he abused me. I was almost five years old. I immediately went in the house and related the events to my father. I didn't understand his rage but the teenage boy did when my father confronted him. We never visited the neighborhood again until after Dad died. This "secret" has never been related to my extended family or my children.

My father and mother are buried beside each other in Greenville and only a stone's throw from a local mill worker, who became a famous baseball player, Shoeless Joe Jackson. Jackson was an illiterate who was involved in baseball's Black Sox scandal. I always wondered how a person could help his team lose games and have the highest batting average of anyone in that World Series.

In summary, my grandfather was an alcoholic who murdered his mistress and was himself murdered. My grandmother died of cancer. The entire family worked at the J. P. Stevens Dunean Plant, a cotton mill in Greenville, until Dad and his brother Quinton became ministers. The entire family, including children and grandchildren, attended and were members of the Dunean Baptist Church .

Robert, the oldest son, was a deacon there. J.B., the black sheep of the family, was a member and probably an alcoholic. Quentin became a Baptist minister. Rama married a Church of God minister. Lucille the last sister, and her husband were lifelong Church of God members. My father became a Church of God minister. Alcohol, strict corporal punishment (spare the rod and spoil the child), abuse, strict fundamentalist churches, diabetes, hypertension, strokes, and secrets were rampant, but our religious faith and the truth of God's forgiveness kept us going.

CHAPTER 2

My mother's family came from the northeastern part of Louisiana. My grandfather, Thomas Horace Morse, married Lucy Walker and they had four children. Mother's family was different from Dad's only in the number of brothers and sisters.

Mother's oldest sister, Maudell, was a very strong woman and was a lifelong Church of God member along with her husband Paul. Paul had a nursery business and they moved to Sarasota, Florida. She eventually was the caretaker for her mother and father and moved them to Sarasota to live with her. They lived in a small house adjacent to hers at the nursery that she and Paul owned.

She had three children late in life. Betty Ann, their oldest daughter, became a schoolteacher and married a school teacher—she is bipolar or manic-depressive. Her brother, my cousin Norman Paul, made it out to California. While there he appeared in several commercials for Dentine chewing gum and became entangled in drugs and bad marriages. He also was bipolar. The youngest daughter was Mary Evelyn. She was named Evelyn after my mother, and was born much later and just after Maudelle found she was diabetic during the pregnancy. Since she was not treated for diabetes, Mary Evelyn was a slow learner and always cared for by her sister Betty Ann. As a physician, I had several conversations with my cousin Betty Ann about her manic depression. She always loved the mania, or high, but could not tolerate the depression. I remember the last time she visited me in Jamestown, Tennessee. She had bought a new RV in Thomasville, Georgia, and had driven it up to Jamestown. After all the small talk and catching up, I asked Betty Ann how long she had been off her medication. She asked "How did you know?" I responded as I was taught in medical school—with a question, "Does your medicine make you feel like a zombie?" Again her response was "How did you know?" I did not tell her that I was well versed with a bipolar diagnosis from my experience with number two, my second wife. Most manic depressive patients love the high but don't fear the depression enough to regularly take medication. I have always believed that if we could have force fed medication daily to the bipolar members of my family and number two, our lives could have been improved. However, most patients respond that they don't like the "zombielike feeling," that the medication brings but makes them appear normal to the rest of us. They tend to stay off medication and tolerate the depression just for the high.

Mother's oldest brother Raymond was a Church of God minister who had two children, both of whom had drug and marital problems. His son became a minister and missionary to Jamaica. He married a local girl and had one daughter. Since then he has had at least two other marriages and at least two other daughters. Raymond's daughter has a longtime marriage and three daughters. Uncle Raymond moved from Louisiana to South Carolina, then to northern Georgia, then to Tennessee. He pastored a small church in Lenoir City, Tennessee, that my father moved to after he left as president of Lee College in 1957.

The sister just older than Mother was Odine. She had a darker complexion and different personality. Although there were many theories proposed for these differences, that was a family secret I was never able to expose. However, she was a lovely lady who never married. At nineteen years old, she was able to move to South Carolina for work and school. My mother joined her several months later. Odine worked for a Church of God minister and as a member of the Church of God Missions Department she served as a missionary to the island of Haiti. She remained there for thirty-three years, lived in the poorest section of

Port au Prince, and spoke fluent Creole. I remember the story of when my father and mother went to Haiti while Dad was President of Lee College in 1952 or 1953.

When Dad flew into the island of Haiti, he had to go through customs. He never could understand why he was shuttled through customs so quickly. Only when Odine was able to catch up with him after customs was she able to explain. Dad bore a remarkable resemblance to Red Skelton and Mr. Skelton was coming to the island in the next few weeks. The airport officials thought Dad was Red Skelton and rushed him through customs. Everyone had a good laugh.

I was able to assist both Odine and my mother after my dad passed away in 1972. Odine had not lived in the United States and had paid no income tax for this period of time. When she returned to Cleveland after spending thirty-three years as a missionary in Haiti, she went to work for the Mission Department. She received a small pension which my father had helped set up as an assistant general overseer of the Church of God. Her total income and pension left her below the poverty level. She could not buy health insurance. It was necessary for me to spend $11,000 for her to "buy in" to the Medicare and Medicaid systems. Many years later she and Mother moved to Jamestown, Tennessee, and eventually to a nursing home located just behind Jamestown Regional Medical Center and about 50 yards from my office.

Odine also had maturity onset diabetes and when I visited her in the nursing home, I would occasionally take a 1 pound bag of M&Ms to her and watch her eyes light up. She loved M&Ms, and salt-and-vinegar potato chips. I figured if she had made it this far, she should enjoy some smaller pleasures. Medicaid also gave her $30 a month while she was in the nursing home for "incidentals." She would take her money each month and make frequent trips to the potato chip and candy machines. Since most of her money was stolen either by residents or staff, I asked that the nursing home hold her money. I brought her chips and M&Ms and paid for her weekly trips to the hairdresser. She had always been a "purple-haired lady" who had her hair done weekly and washed with whatever shampoo they used to make white hair purple. She passed away less than a year before my mother.

Mother was the fourth child and the baby of the family, born when her mother Lucy was forty-four years old. My mother's first name was Linus. She was named after one of her uncles on her mother's side. I used to kid mother about her (Linus) and her mother (Lucy) being the first characters that led to the comic strip *Peanuts*. My grandmother's maiden name was Walker and she had four brothers all of whom were 6 feet 4 inches or taller, all developed thick white hair and arthritis of their hands as they grew older, and lived into their late nineties. That sort of describes me at the present time genetically. At seventy-five years of age and having just attended my fiftieth year medical school reunion, I appear to have done very well—genetically speaking, of course. At the time mother went to high school, there were only eleven grades as there were with my father's high school. She moved to South Carolina to live with her sister in Greenville and it was there that she met my father. Mother then married my father just before he became a Church of God minister. After Dad passed away, Mother lived in Cleveland, Tennessee, where my three oldest children lived. She had essentially raised my oldest son's youngest daughter. She would babysit her, read books, and sing songs to her. Mother had bought a duplex that she eventually gifted to me and my wife, Cindy. Mother and I always had the agreement that she could live alone until I needed to move her to be with me. Approximately two years before she moved to Jamestown, she fell and fractured her hip. She went to rehabilitation in Cleveland. Mother then fell while in her bathroom, causing a large laceration to her forehead. I felt that she could no longer take care of herself and with her in full agreement, moved her to my home in Jamestown. While she stayed with us, she actually stayed in our bedroom and we moved our bed to the living room. She had episodes of moaning and groaning during the night and we were unable to arouse her. After several trips to the emergency room, we discovered she occasionally had a very low blood sugar. We adjusted her diet but to no avail. She frequently required IV fluids with 50 percent dextrose. I felt that she had an insulinoma, a tumor which is found in the pancreatic gland and causes massive amounts of insulin to be secreted. When I discussed the possibility with her, she asked what it would take to diagnose and treat this condition. I told her that it would take a CT scan and, if positive, would possibly require surgery. She refused the workup and stated that she would not permit any surgery. It became obvious that we could not take care of her at home. After several months, we transferred her to the nursing home to be with her sister. I'm not sure if she even realized when her sister passed away. About six months later, Mother also passed away. This was about eight months before we moved to Florida.

My mother's family home place in Dunn, Louisiana, consisted of a six-room house with three bedrooms, kitchen, living room and dining room, screen doors in front and back, and a large front porch with a swing. Later an indoor bathroom was added. The house itself was covered with tarpaper for insulation and over this, aged wood planks. The home had inside gas lights and an ice box before electricity was added. There was a barn with stalls for the horses and cows and hay. The washer was in the barn next to where the cows were milked. An electric wire was brought from the house to the barn for the washer. There was also a single lightbulb if needed at night. The washer also had the first step in drying, a wringer. The dryer was several clotheslines outside in the backyard. I saw several "degloving" injuries of the skin from attempts to pull out a trapped finger, hand, or arm that had been inadvertently caught while pushing wet clothes through the two rollers of the wringer. Later models were improved and had a release bar below the two rollers. When hit, the bar caused the rollers to separate and the caught part could be easily removed. This release mechanism drastically reduced injuries.

Initially there was only a two-seater outhouse that had a container on each side with corn cobs for cleaning yourself (four brown cobs followed by a white cob to check your progress) and later a Sears and Roebuck catalog for reading material or wiping. A bathtub, sink, and inside plumbing was finally added. There were forty fenced acres of flat pastureland with maybe five cows.

The town of Dunn had a population of maybe one hundred. There was a general store that included basic groceries, a gas station, and a post office. The forty acres of land my grandfather owned were on the other side of the railroad tracks which were across the highway and ran parallel to the stores. I don't think much has changed over the past seventy years. There are no census numbers for Dunn, but the area is said to include two small villages.

For the first seven to eight years of my life, we visited my grandparents irregularly but at least once a year. I watched cows being fed and milked by hand. I could never understand why the cows were killed by hitting them in the head with a hammer and the pigs were shot in the head with a .22 rifle. Only the pigs were strung up in a tree. Their throats were cut to remove the blood. Sausage making was a family affair. I watched the pig meat being ground up and placed in the casings made of pig intestines.

Grandma let me churn cow's milk in a one-gallon square glass container which had four paddles for churning that you turned by hand. It was hard work but I enjoyed watching the fresh cow's milk quickly become butter after turning the paddles for what seemed like forever. Even better was spreading that fresh butter on gingerbread or some hot homemade biscuits. I think I was the only grandchild for whom Grandma made gingerbread.

My grandfather was a Singer sewing machine salesman. He also dabbled in local and state politics and was a Huey Long "chicken in every pot" Democrat. I heard him say that many times but never understood what it meant. Grandma was hard-headed and opinionated but never saw the need for voting. I think she did it just to spite my grandpa. He drove a 1948 Studebaker and never went anywhere unless his left front and rear tires were on the centerline of the highway. He dared other cars to make him move. Grandpa, Grandma, and Mother sat in the front seat and I had to sit in the middle of the backseat to "balance the load."

One of my fondest childhood memories was of going to the cattle auctions in Delhi, Louisiana, with my grandpa. I had no idea what the auctioneer was saying or how any of the participants made bids on the cows but I enjoyed the entire atmosphere. The cows would enter the ring and were herded around in front of the prospective buyers by "cowboys" using electric prods. Each of the cows had a tag on one of their ears for identification. Sometimes there was a lot of commotion from the bulls and a cowboy would rapidly scamper up the heavy metal retaining fences. The cows were then herded out the side and loaded in the waiting trucks of their new owners. Grandpa rarely bought anything but I still enjoyed the action. I asked my grandfather to take me every opportunity that I was with him.

Grandpa taught me to drink coffee at about four years of age. He would "saucer" his coffee to let it cool and left some of the coffee with cream and sugar in his cup for me to discover and drink. He would mix all his food together on the same plate before he ate. At breakfast, he added syrup over his bacon, eggs, pancakes, and grits before eating. I also remember my grandfather had a very large inguinal hernia and that he wore a "truss." At the time I never understood anything about that condition or treatment.

Mother would take the old Studebaker and use it while we were visiting. I was told that when I was about one year old and was standing in the front seat between Mother, who was driving, and Odine, who was sitting beside the door, Mother had corrected me for something and I reached back to hit her with my fist. She replied, "Don't you do that!" so I turned around and clobbered my Aunt Odine on the shoulder. I was not corrected and both thought it was very funny.

My grandmother had cut her left thumb flexor tendon and could not bring her thumb toward her hand. Nevertheless, she taught me to tie my shoes when I was four. It was fascinating to watch her do this without the use of her left thumb. She "potty-trained" me by allowing me to run around naked outside. One of the first complete sentences I uttered was "Go way fly, pee-pee nasty."

I spent many lonely hours in Dunn. Most of the time I spent alone unless some of the rest of the family was there with kids. It's difficult to play baseball by yourself, and the only things I remember doing were hitting a tennis ball with a flat wooden shingle and flying a balsa wood airplane that was launched by a large rubber band. Even though there were not a lot of things to do, the grownups seemed to have a good time reminiscing and telling stories.

No one in Mom's family drank whiskey at all. They all attended a small Pentecostal church within a half mile of the homestead. Mother later told me memories of church services there. A young girl was "in the spirit" and placed her entire head and long blonde hair inside a potbellied coal stove used for heating the church. Neither she nor her hair were burned. On one occasion, a snake-handling minister came to town and to the small church that the family attended. My mother stated that this had never happened before or since, but when she saw the snakes brought out, she was frightened and dove under the front pew. The minister with the snakes was bitten in the arm and the venom from the rattlesnake caused his arm to swell massively. He almost died but slowly improved over the next few days while he lived on the front porch of my grandparents' house. Dad rarely stayed in Louisiana when Mom and I went for a visit. I guess he was ministering or working on his education, but I never discovered the reason why. Secret?

Many times the only vacation we had was visiting and staying with family in South Carolina, Louisiana, or Florida.

CHAPTER 3

One of the first secrets of Dad and Mother's life was not telling anyone they had eloped to get married. They only relented because of the real possibility that Mother would get pregnant before they told anyone they were married. That would have been much more difficult to explain than just telling the truth.

Mom and Dad always wanted several children. There is only one way I can explain why I was an only child. Mother had a ruptured appendix the year after I was born. Many medical advances take place in the years after a war. In 1942 there were few or no antibiotics. In fact during the war, penicillin was used as a new medication and was often extracted back from the urine of the patient on whom it was used. Sulfa was also a new drug and had limited uses. Surgery was the only treatment for appendicitis. Sometimes the operation did not adequately remove the entire infection. The residual infection could cause much scarring in the abdomen and pelvis and close the fallopian tubes, preventing the tubes from functioning correctly and resulting in sterility.

When I was born, I was named Ramon Leonard Carroll, Junior. Later when my father checked his birth certificate for college, he realized that it showed the name Ramon Leonard Livingston Carroll and theoretically I was not a junior. He had to go to court and have his name changed by taking out the name Livingston. Only then did I officially become a junior. I kept that nickname "Junior" throughout my first ten

15

years in South Carolina. When I changed schools and started the fifth grade at Arnold Memorial School in Cleveland, Tennessee, the nickname "Junior" was dropped from use except for church and family members. It's embarrassing now for an old friend to use that name in a conversation with others who have never heard it. I did not like the sound or the sarcasm old "friends" used when pronouncing it. I hated the name "Junior" and wanted to be called Leonard as my father was.

I always wondered why my father's first name was Ramon (pronounced ray-mon) instead of Raymond. One of my dad's older sisters was named Rama. When we moved to Clewiston, Florida, eleven years ago, I met a male nurse from Puerto Rico who worked with me in surgery. His name was Ramon (with the Spanish pronunciation) Soto. I had watched my father put butter between saltine crackers and soak them in strong, black coffee. I was really surprised when Ramon did the same thing one morning before surgery started. My dad's name being Ramon, his sister's name being Rama, and the dunking of saltine crackers and butter in coffee made me wonder if there were some Hispanic family secrets that I could never uncover.

Dad pastored churches in Chester, Greer, and Anderson, South Carolina. I was ten months old when I began walking while Dad pastored a small church in Chester. Mother had just baked biscuits in the oven of an old porcelain stove. I was in the kitchen with her when I toddled over, stumbled, and fell on the side of the stove. The surface, of course, was extremely hot. I jerked back and fell again on the side of the stove. Each time I landed on my outstretched hands and burned the palms of both my hands. I had deep second-degree burns. Our house in Chester was a mill house and was close enough to the neighbors to talk to them through the screened open windows. Mother screamed for help and the neighbors got in touch with my father. I was taken to a general practitioner who for some reason only treated my right hand with ointment and bandages. Within two days it was obvious from the large blisters that both of my palms were burned badly. They took me back to the doctor who then treated both hands. He warned my parents that since there were no antibiotics to use, there could be severe infection and scarring. Mom and Dad did what they knew how to do best. My parents called the entire congregation of the small church and they and the church prayed for my healing. When I visited the same doctor a week after the burns, my hands were completely healed. He said my hands were "soft as a baby's butt"—a total impossibility! I reached the same conclusion by the many burns I have treated in my life. I was healed and given my hands for use then and for use later as a surgeon. Was this a miracle or just coincidence? It was a miracle no doubt.

My first memories of my dad were when I was about three years old standing beside him in the front seat of our car and reading his books to him. I didn't know most of the words but he would very patiently correct my pronunciation and explain what the words meant. I guess you could say he taught me to read.

There was an occasion about this time that Dad and Mother and I went to Atlanta, Georgia to visit one of Dad's friends, Lloyd Robbins. It seemed like everything he touched "turned to gold." Every business he associated himself with succeeded. His oldest daughter took me to see a large concrete fish pond in the front yard of her house. I was about four years old and she was about eight years of age. For some reason she shoved me into the pond. I almost drowned before they pulled me out. Miracle or coincidence? Later she became a patient of mine.

In 1948 again we were visiting with Mr. Robbins on a Saturday afternoon when I saw the first television set I had ever seen. The television was approximately four feet high, eighteen inches deep, and approximately three feet wide. There was an eight inch circular screen in the middle and upper part of the front and the colors on the screen were brown and white. The only programming came from Chicago. Both Mr. Robbins and my father were amazed that someone could take pictures broadcast in Chicago, throw them through the air until they were caught, and we were able to see them on the television set. He was a wealthy man but I wonder what that first television set cost him.

We moved to Greer and again lived in a parsonage that the church

17

owned, across the street from the small church Dad pastored. This was true of all the churches Dad pastored. I had my first experience of being bitten by another child there. The first time was by a cousin who was my age. We were looking out of a window into the backyard when she bit me. She screamed so loudly that everyone rushed to her and assumed that I had bitten her. Only when I showed my mother the teeth marks on my arm was the culprit identified. A visiting Armenian minister's daughter about my age bit me shortly after that incident and my dad had had enough. He had a talk with me and said that I should bite back if anyone bit me again. I never did because I feared the other fathers.

There was a small grocery store across the street from our house and next to the church. My mother would call the grocery store or I would carry a list to get the groceries she needed. Dad's salary was not very good and we could not have eaten regularly except the grocery owner allowed us to carry a bill and pay him when we could, usually monthly and I'm sure at a discount. This was one of the first times I remember a business giving my father and our family "professional courtesy". When I was later in medical practice, I always tried to return the favors done for my family by returning care to ministers and their families for free or as a "professional courtesy".

I remember an old black gentleman coming to our back door, knocking, and asking for something to eat. He stood outside with his hat in his hands. My mother gave him the same thing she was eating—a tomato and lettuce sandwich with mayonnaise on white bread. He thanked her profusely.

The only other time I remember even seeing black men was when the city garbage collectors came to our house. They backed the truck up beside the house and went around back to pick up our garbage can. I was afraid of most visitors, especially the black garbage collectors, and would crawl under the kitchen table. Once when the garbage collectors arrived and I was trying to hide, I jumped off the bench at our kitchen table and hit the edge of the wooden table and got my first laceration just above the left eye. I was lucky—no stitches.

We were visiting the family of one of the church members who lived on a farm. I saw my first Ferris wheel. The father had made a wooden Ferris wheel about eight feet tall with four seats. It was hooked to his tractor motor to make it turn. I was too afraid to ride it.

I also had my first real punishment. I "ran off" from my house and went around the corner out of sight to another house without telling my parents. They looked for me for quite a while before I was found playing with other kids. My father had brought a switch (forsythia switches were the worst) with him. I saw him and started running. It seemed as if he hit my legs every step of the way as I ran back home. I never ran away again and to this day I tell everyone, at home or even at my office, where I'm going each time I leave.

It was about this time that I had the most unusual experience I've ever had. I don't remember any crisis in the family before or after the event. As far as I remember, times were good. Dad and I were riding in an old two-door coupe along a dirt road. It was dusk when he pulled off the side of the road and told me to get out of the car. I didn't want to. He kept telling me to get out and eventually I did. He drove off and I "cried my eyes out". It seemed like forever but he finally came back, opened the door, and I got in. I had never moved from where I had gotten out. This secret was never mentioned again until about forty years later when I was treated for codependency. In the treatment I was told that most of the problems in my life had originated from that "abandonment" by my father and then never talking about it.

I don't understand why the "abandonment" happened but I do believe with all my heart Ephesians 6:1–3 that states, "Children, obey your parents in the Lord: for this is right. Honour thy father and mother; (which is the first commandment with promise) that it may be well with thee, and thou mayest live long on the earth." I wish I had worked it out before Dad passed away but I didn't. I have asked God's forgiveness for my feelings since then. I never forgave my father until after he died. Even then it was difficult.

Chapter 4

We moved to Anderson when I was five years old and remained there for about five years. We lived in another mill house called a "shotgun house" for the first three years. Again, all the houses were essentially the same size and shape. Each house had a front porch, dirt yard (no grass), a central hall with one front bedroom on the right and one bedroom in the back on the left. The living room was on the left, the dining room in the middle on the right, and the kitchen on the right in the back. The bathroom was on the left part of the back porch. The small back porch on the right had steps down to the backyard which was used for work. There was a clothesline on the left side of the back-yard. Again there was no grass, only packed dirt. Dad's contribution to a chicken dinner was converting live chickens to dead ones. He was an expert on wringing chicken necks. After this happened, they flopped all over the yard. Then were hung by their feet on the clothesline where their heads were cut off and blood drained out. Sometimes after their legs were tied, you could hold the chicken with one hand and lay it on an old tree stump, and then use an axe to cut off its head. Mom had a large pot of hot water where she placed the chicken after all the feathers had been plucked off. The hot water was for soaking and removing the pin feathers. I can still remember the smell. Every time the dentist is grinding out a cavity, I'm reminded of that smell. We lived right across the street from a public school with a large playground behind it. I watched my father kick a ball so high in the air that I could hardly see it. He was my hero.

When I turned five years old, I was a head taller than most other kids. My dad had encouraged my learning by asking questions like, "When did Columbus discover America?" I replied, "1492." Then he would ask, "When were you born?" I answered, "1942." Sometimes I got the dates reversed which would make everyone laugh, except me. I already could read and write. Dad thought I was ready to go to school the next school year. There was only one problem: the city school board would not let me attend a city school until I was six. Dad talked to Mr. Hanks, who was the principal of a county school. Mrs. Hanks, his wife, taught the first grade. They agreed to let me attend this country school. Every morning my dad would take me to the outskirts of town to a gas station where I would wait for the school bus (a pickup with the back covered with a canvas tarp over the top and benches on either side). I didn't realize it but in this county school, the first four grades were taught all in the same classroom. The first graders were to sit quietly after their teaching while the second, third, and fourth grades were being taught. I didn't know any difference and just learned it all. I listened and learned everything. I'm still waiting for someone to ask me the first twenty-six counties in South Carolina in alphabetical order. I can do it. Abbeville, Akin, Allendale, Anderson. Bamberg, Barnwell…. I learned to never climb a tree at recess unless I knew I had time to get down if the bell rang to end recess. I loved my brown bag lunches, usually a peanut butter and grape jelly sandwich. I learned three ways to open a bottle of Coca Cola without a bottle opener: shaking it until the top popped off (you had to be very fast to place your thumb over the top of the bottle after doing this), use your teeth (which I never learned to do), and use the edge of a wooden desk by placing the crimped bottle top on the edge of the desk and striking it with the heel of your hand. I learned to write cursive and continued to read. After school, I would ride the school bus/pickup truck back to the service station and wait until Mom or Dad picked me up. I learned to love the smell of new tires that were usually stacked up in front of the station.

My dad expressed to me at an early age that the only chance of my success was getting an education. He proved it to me by beginning his own education. He was twenty-two years old when I was born. He went to Wofford College in Spartanburg, which was close to Greenville. It required him to drive to the train station each morning to commute. In winter, with freezing temperatures, he had to drain the water from his car's radiator to prevent it from bursting while the car was sitting at the train station all day. He would then catch the train for school. When he returned from school it would usually be dark. He would then have to put water back in the radiator of his car to drive home. After a year, he attended Furman University in Greenville, South Carolina, and obtained his BA degree.

Mom always wanted a house of her own—not one that the church provided. Dad bought a white asbestos shingled house at 3100 Edgewood Avenue. The house was on a large corner lot. This was the only house we ever owned. We lived across the street from a Jewish couple who owned the local jewelry store, lived in a brick house, and had three kids. I learned the joys of Charlie's Chips and M&M's in large metal cans. I remember when I found out that all the colored M&M's were chocolate inside and not just the brown ones. They gave me the best birthday gift I ever got—a zippered billfold with a cowboy on one side and a horse's head on the other side. I kept it for years.

There was a contest down at a local hardware store in Anderson that had a Christmas promotion. You could register to win a large Lionel train set. I begged and pleaded with my parents to just take me to the store and let me register in the contest. After all, the train could make smoke and had a horn that you could blow. They relented, I registered, and my name was drawn. That Christmas I had a large Lionel train set to enjoy that I would never have gotten any other way. Many years later, number two "twisted my arm" and had me give the train to her uncle who collected trains.

I also remember the Buster Brown Shoe store which had a machine that you could step up on and slide your feet under. You could actually see through your shoes and watch your toes, or at least the bones in your toes, wiggle inside your shoes. I had no idea what these machines were as did none of the other kids or moms. We would stand for five or ten minutes at a time with our feet placed under the machine and wiggle our toes. I think it was used to make sure your shoes were large enough for future growth. The machine was left unattended and there was no one there to supervise. So we spent a lot of time playing at this machine. I realized after using a fluoroscopy machine in my medical training and in my practice that the Buster Brown shoe sizing machine was a fluoroscope. There was a viewing port on the top that you could look in to see how your shoes fit your feet. There were two more ports on each side so your parents or other kids could watch you wiggle your toes inside your shoes. This machine was actually an X-ray unit. The part of the fluoroscopy unit that created the X-rays was at the same level as my lower abdomen and testicles. It was only after World War II and medical follow-up on long-term atomic bomb victims that you could see the effects of radiation with burns and sterility in some of the survivors.

These machines were eventually taken out of shoe stores because they actually didn't help with sizing of your shoes. Maybe someone thought of the possible problems. Wonder if those things ever caused any damage to future generations? Maybe that's why all my sons are close to six feet tall. I'm sure there would be multiple lawsuits if such machines were used in department stores today. I bet you could find one of these on eBay or possibly in a museum somewhere.

Dad was an innovator and always enjoyed new technology when it originally came out. I remember him buying and using a self-contained unit which included both a radio (on which I remember listening to my first New York Yankees baseball game in 1949) and a recording device that actually cut grooves in a vinyl disc or record. All this was for home use. I remember recording several conversations at home with him, my mother, and me. And I also made my singing debut and still have that first vinyl record. I guess I was an original one-hit wonder, at least in my family.

I found out later that one of the reasons we moved was so I could go to the city school system in the second grade. There, I learned to print instead of continuing to write cursive. I now use my printing sort of like italics when I'm taking notes. I don't remember much of the second, third, or fourth grades except I began having migraine headaches. Several times I had had to sit on the curb by the roadside and wait until my mother eventually found me and brought me home. Later in life, the only way I could manage migraine headaches was by "sticking my finger down my throat" in order to vomit. This would give me several hours of relief, would take away the nausea, and lessen the headache. In medical school I found a wonderful drug called Valium. This always relieved the headache and put me to sleep.

I remember getting bitten by a friend's dog as I tried to pet it with my foot. The bite was not treated. We seldom went to the doctor. Mother's remedy was "feed a cold and starve a fever." I never really enjoyed the hot water and lemon juice that she made me drink like tea. I didn't mind "milk toast" which was one piece of toasted white bread that was put in hot buttered milk and soaked until the bread was soft. I also remember getting regular doses of castor oil. This was good for everything from a stomach ache to constipation.

My mother was always there when I came home from school. I could tell her everything that had happened that day. She was a "talker" who could take a question and spend thirty minutes answering it. We used to call it "going around your elbow to get to your mouth." All of my life I remember interrupting her to ask that she hurry up and get to the point of whatever we were discussing. She usually took my side and tried to talk Dad out of many of the whippings I got but I never remember it ever getting me out of a whipping. Mother was a stay-at-home mom or "homemaker" and I always appreciated that.

My best friend while growing up was Tommy Wilson. I remember watching wrestling on a black-and-white large-floor model television set at his neighbor's house (they were also church members). There was always a distinction between the "good guys" and the "bad guys."

Wrestlers included the Smith Brothers; Gorgeous George, who had golden blond hair with gold-colored bobby pins in his hair; Hombre Montana; and the Alligator Man. Wrestling was obviously fake but was very exciting. It was almost more fun to watch little old ladies in the audience on TV who would hit the wrestlers with folding chairs or see a young woman use the heel of her high heeled shoe on the wrestler's head. Our mothers yelled and screamed at the TV wrestling action also. All the kids would gather in front of the TV while our parents sat behind us. Once "Pickle" Campbell's mother and father were sitting on the couch while we were watching wrestling and his father evidently had his arm around his wife and accidentally or purposefully touched her chest. She asked if he was looking for a "fried egg," took out a falsie, and threw it at him. I never figured out if this had anything to do with wrestling or what else it could've meant. We kids continued watching TV, but Pickle and his sister were totally embarrassed.

Mother and Dad had taken me to spend the night with Tommy Wilson while they went out of town. My parents arrived back in town about 2:00 AM. They came over to the Wilson's house and woke everyone up and took me home. I never understood that.

We didn't have a TV then so I listened to a lot of radio. I didn't have a watch, but could tell every afternoon when it was five o'clock. I knew it was time to run home to listen to *The Lone Ranger*. Saturday mornings included *Big John and Sparkie* and *No School Today*. Does anyone else remember "Plunk your magic twanger, Froggy"? My imagination was much better than any TV I ever watched, and it was in color, too.

I continued to go with my father to many ministerial functions he performed, including marriages, funerals, and baptizings. I was baptized at five years of age. It happened when my father took a young man out to a local lake to be baptized and I followed both out into the water. I would not be deterred and asked my father to immerse me also. He did. Afterwards Dad and I talked about "giving my heart to Jesus" and living for Him. This was a crucial day in my life. I also believe this was the beginning of my difficulties in separating my heavenly Father from my earthly father. I discovered an amazing fact: it is a very simple thing to become a Christian. First, you must believe that Jesus Christ is the only begotten son of God. Second, believe that He came to earth as a man and died on the cross for our sins. Third, accept Him as Savior. Fourth, ask Him to come in your life. The results are eternal life, unless I remove myself from His hand. This has been the glue that has held my life and my family's life together.

Corporal punishment began at this time also. Since our church had services Wednesday night, Saturday night Y.P.E. (Young People's Endeavor), a separate Sunday morning service with Sunday School and preaching, and another service at night on Sunday, I felt I was always in church. If services got long, I was allowed to lie down on the pew. Many times I went to sleep. This practice stopped when I started taking up over half of the pew when I laid down. The extra time in church caused a lot of "cutting up" or rowdiness and, of course, frequent whippings.

Some amazing things happened during church. One elderly gentleman in our church threatened to cut off my ears. I would always hide when I saw him coming. Most of the others just laughed. Dad said he was kidding and I should tolerate it. I couldn't.

Most people were very respectful in church and followed the biblical guideline of men keeping their heads uncovered while in church. Hats were removed and placed on the pew beside the men or hung on coatracks in the back of the church. Women could wear hats, mostly on special occasions, but again their heads were usually uncovered. This is very different from today when even baseball caps are worn during church services.

The church even had rules about people who disagreed with the teachings and caused disruption. Once when about one third of the membership decided my father was trying to move the church in the wrong direction, certain steps were instituted. This included bringing "charges" against the dissenters in an open meeting. If the problems could not be resolved, the people were "turned out", and most would leave the church and go elsewhere, probably to start another church with people who believed like them. I noticed that husbands and wives who were married and stayed together for many years usually passed away within six months of each other.

I personally observed some unusual things. I saw a young man who was "in the spirit" walk from the pointed end of one pew to the pointed end of the next pew. He then stepped across the aisle and walked back up the other side, stepping from one pew to the next. All of this was with his eyes closed. There was "speaking in tongues" and interpretations. People were "slain in the spirit" and fell immediately to the floor. This still happens in the church I now attend. I assume that is where the term "holy rollers" came from. Have you ever looked under the pews in the first few front rows? You better be "slain in the spirit" because there are chewing gum and other nasal unmentionables stuck there. Or they were the last time I looked.

The church seemed to always have troubles financially. The ladies decided to do something about the problem. They formed a group called the Ladies Willing Worker's Band, or LWWB for short. I remember them taking meals consisting of fried chicken, mashed potatoes, green beans, and a roll, usually prepared in the kitchen in the basement of the church, out to local mills and businesses. They sold these lunches for one dollar and, of course, that included a glass of sweetened iced tea. They made a lot of money for the church.

There were few restaurants in the forties in small towns. One local restaurant, or grill, in Anderson was The Greasy Spoon. The owners actually had a sign hanging in front of the restaurant that consisted of a large spoon with three drops of grease dripping from it, all outlined in neon tubing, including the three drops of grease. They had great hamburgers. You could actually see the grill with hamburgers and hot dogs cooking in the front window. One day I changed my usual eating habits. I saw an order of spaghetti and meatballs and I told Dad that was what I wanted. He said it was too much for me but I persisted. It wasn't like what my mother cooked and I couldn't eat it all. Dad forced me to eat it and it all came back up in the car later. I got two whippings—one for not eating what I said I wanted, and one for vomiting in the car.

There were many arguments between my parents, and some of them got very loud and heated. There was never any physical abuse. The mental abuse made me promise at the time that this would never happen to me as an adult. However, they became patterns for me to follow in my adult life. Most of my parents' problems were related to finance, church situations, and problems with both sides of the family. Many times these arguments occurred in the car on trips to visit family, and they seemed to last forever. It made me want to avoid these kinds of disagreements. I learned to shut out the arguments and avoid reality usually by reading or if we were at home, I would just stay in my room.

Most Sunday mornings after church, the members would invite the minister and his family out to their homes for dinner. As you would guess, it was for fried chicken, mashed potatoes, green beans, and rolls or biscuits. One positive thing came out of that and I learned it very early. The kids had to eat in the kitchen and that was usually where all the desserts, cakes, or pies were kept. I began a lifelong problem of being overweight. I promised myself that once I "grew up," I would never eat fried chicken, mashed potatoes, or green beans again. I continued with the desserts. In the country we had breakfast, dinner, and supper for our three meals. I still have difficulty now calling them breakfast, lunch, and dinner.

The very small front yard at the mill house we lived in was packed-down dirt. The sidewalk was elevated at the front of the house and there was a large tree next to the sidewalk. I devised a trapeze from a low hanging strong limb and used rope to attach to both sides of a broomstick for the trapeze bar. A nail had been driven into the broomstick and was unnoticed by me as it stuck out only slightly. While jumping from the sidewalk, I was able to grab the trapeze bar and swing into the yard. On one of many jumps, I let loose and the nail head ripped a large laceration in the skin of my left middle finger. It was on the palmar aspect of my finger, crossed two joints, and caused a lot of bleeding. My left hand was wrapped up in clean rags and due to the severity of the injury, I was taken to the local hospital Emergency Room. I still have a picture in my mind of lying on the examining table while my wound was irrigated with hydrogen peroxide. The nurse had allowed my dad to come just inside the double doors to wait. As they began to explore the wound and look for tendon damage, the pain increased. I began to cry and complain but my father just looked at me very sternly from the corner of the room and mouthed to me, "Don't cry." Immediately I knew it would be better for me to not continue crying. A doctor and nurse stood on each side of my arm to prevent me from seeing what was going on, but I had a good view between them and watched everything they did. I was told what a "good boy" I was. This encouraged my hiding my emotions. Within the next few days my father took off my bandage and the entire finger was swollen and pus was coming out between the stitches. He took a sewing needle and sterilized it in the flame of a match and used it to drain the "laudable pus." My finger healed well with no complications. When the doctor removed the sutures, he said "You're really lucky to have no problems or tendon damage." Coincidence or a miracle?

Another time we were playing at a neighbor's house in an old car with running boards. One of the other kids slammed the door on my bare foot and my left great toenail was pried off, causing a lot of pain and bleeding. Again there were no antibiotics or money to go the doctor, so the wound was wrapped and several days later became red and infected. My dad again sterilized a needle and while sitting on the front steps of the church, he drained the pus from my toe. It then healed with no complications. Many times my father mentioned that he had wanted to become a medical doctor before he was called to the ministry.

Diphtheria, three-day measles, the big measles, whooping cough, and chickenpox were common. When their kids got measles or chicken pox, mothers actually had parties and other kids were invited to the infected kid's house so that they would hopefully catch the virus. I guess this was their form of controlled inoculation. Smallpox injections were given to everyone when school started. One of my best friends had had diphtheria as a much younger child, and had a permanent metal tracheostomy tube. It didn't slow him down. He could run and play like the rest of us and talked in a wheezing fashion when he held his finger over the top of the tracheostomy tube. He could also pull the inner cannula out and sling phlegm, or "snot" on any of his enemies. He could "cuss" better than any kid I've ever known. I learned words I never repeated. I read the entire section of H's in the dictionary looking for the word *whore* and learned how to spell *damn* with an N. I was taught that "cussing" was bad. Dad told me I would never need to "cuss." He told me to use my head and not stupid "cuss words." One thing was for sure: if I used God's name in vain, I would die and go to hell and would get a whipping too.

My friend's mother and father both worked. They had a large farm outside Anderson, South Carolina. His father also owned a radiator repair shop in town, close to the Buster Brown shoe store. Mother, Dad, and I visited with the family frequently and had many homecooked country meals including vegetables that they had "canned" or "put up" at the end of summer. Their family was almost completely self-sufficient. They had cows, pigs, and other animals. I think the guineas that roosted in a large tree next to the house were the original home security alarm system because they made a horrible noise when anyone came up to the house. Even the small amounts of vegetables that were left over after canning, including corn, green beans, potatoes, and tomatoes were placed together and made a great vegetable soup which was especially good with homemade cornbread on cold winter nights. They even had a "canning" machine that would join a metal lid to a tin can by using a hand-operated crimper. "Canning" with cans or using Mason jars for canning was hot hard work. I saw many pressure cooker injuries, most of which happened when the pressure cooker exploded. Burns were common, along with being hit in the head with the flying top of the pressure cooker.

One occasion in the winter, we went up to the farm. A minister from Canada had come to visit and preach a revival at our church. He wanted to do some hunting, so Dad and I took him to the farm. I never remember my father doing that before. The minister, my father, and I went out

31

together. They used the rifles and ammunition the farmer owned. I was just along for the ride. Dad had rarely used guns and did not recognize the difference between a .22 caliber short bullet and .22 caliber long rifle bullet. My father and the other minister took handfuls of both kinds of ammunition and placed them loosely in their pockets. We had just entered a wooded area when the minister placed a .22 caliber long rifle bullet in his rifle which could only take .22 short bullets. The bullet would not go into the gun and jammed at the entrance of the barrel. My father's friend pulled back the spring-loaded firing pin. He took his pocketknife out and tried to remove the bullet that was stuck. I was standing in front of him close to the barrel. While manipulating the bullet, his hand slipped and the firing pin was engaged and the bullet exploded. Fragments of the sleeve of the bullet were embedded in his right eye. We placed him in our car and rushed him to the hospital. He was transferred to a larger hospital where they were able to perform eye surgery. After surgery, he slowly became totally blind in his right eye. Even though I was standing in front of him when the accident occurred, I was not injured. I did hear the bullet whiz past me. Miracle or coincidence?

The next summer, I was enjoying a hot afternoon on the front porch while lying down and swinging on an old metal glider at my friend's house. I had one foot on the porch to push the glider back and forth. My blue jeans were loose and the leg of my jeans hit a nest of hornets under the glider. Several hornets went up my right pants leg and then when I jumped up several others went up the left pants leg. By the time we got home I counted approximately twenty stings on each leg. I remember sitting on the counter in the kitchen while soaking my legs in hot water in the sink. With no EpiPen to use, no Benadryl, no salve, no emergency room visit, what could be done? There was massive swelling of both legs. A lot of prayer and time took care of everything. Miracle or coincidence?

My father made a deal with a local funeral home owner. He would give a donation to the church if my father would have the congregation come to the funeral home after church late on a Sunday night. Everyone who attended got a tour of all the variety of coffins that were there. There was a sealed upright package in a corner which supposedly contained the body of a serviceman who had been sent back from overseas. He had been killed in Germany after World War II and had no one to claim his body. Everyone stayed until after midnight. I think both the funeral home and the church profited from this experience. I know all the kids really enjoyed it. At that time, most of the viewings were done in the home. The coffin was taken in the front door of the house if it was wide enough and if not, through a window. The family would sit up with the body while friends visited. Usually there was a lot of great food brought in by church members. I think people brought food for funerals, weddings, "home-comings," Wednesday night dinners, and any other occasion they could think of. Great time for socializing, telling stories, and good eating.

When I was seven, I went with my father so he could speak at a funeral at another church instead of ours. Instead of going inside, I stayed in the car. I had no idea about car batteries or how easily they could be drained of energy when the radio was left on for any length of time when the car was not running. I quickly learned. While everyone was in church, I listened to a ballgame. Dad's car was parked behind the hearse. When everyone came out of the church, I turned the radio off quickly and acted innocent. It was not funny when the hearse had to use jumper cables to get my dad's car started. Yes—I did receive a whipping when I got home. This had to be one of the most embarrassing experiences I had in my young life to that point. You never counted the number of cars in a funeral procession because that would be the number of years left in your life.

Corporal punishment continued as usual. I can only remember my mother correcting me one time by whipping me with one of her cloth belts. I cried horribly just to make her think it hurt. It was different with Dad. He always sat me down and talked to me. He would pray with me and then take off his leather belt. He would take me by my left hand with his left hand and while holding the belt in his right hand, he would whip me as I ran circles around him, crying the whole time because of the pain. I believe I hated the talks more than the whippings.

I had a nuncupative list of things I couldn't do as a Christian. About a third made sense, about a third I had no idea what they were, and about a third I wanted to do. I was afraid to ask the difference. We prayed before every meal and at bedtime with our eyes closed. I learned that there were ten commandments, not ten suggestions. I learned what keeping a promise meant. My father had promised me a whipping because of something unremembered that had happened in church. I usually hoped he would just forget the incident but true to form he never did. I begged and pleaded not to get a whipping. Dad said, "Since someone has been promised a whipping, then someone has to get a whipping." I was going to be let off the hook this time. But to my dismay, I was told to take off his belt and to whip him. I cried a lot and very feebly gave him a couple of licks with the belt. He demanded that I hit him more and hit him harder. It was difficult to do and I cried the entire time. That was the only time in my life that I remember not getting a promised whipping. Promises are important and binding.

Again, Dad was a visionary. For a new church he bought a wooded lot on a corner in downtown Anderson, South Carolina, across from a beautiful church. He wanted our church to be facing toward the corner when it was eventually built. However, I was able to visit the church as an adult and found that they had placed the new church facing the street rather than toward the corner as Dad had visualized. I learned that church members can be as difficult to deal with as doctors when you're trying to get them to arrive at a conclusion you want.

We moved to Cleveland, Tennessee, in the summer just before I turned ten years old. Due to his formal education, Dad had become president at Lee College in 1952.

CHAPTER 5

At age thirty-two my dad became president of Lee College in Cleveland, Tennessee. I was almost ten years old. When we first moved there and attended a service in the auditorium at the college, I noticed that a large LC was on the curtains behind the podium. I thought the staff had made preparations to celebrate my father's arrival by placing his initials on the stage curtains. I did not realize that the LC stood for Lee College rather than Leonard Carroll. We later moved to Lenoir City in Loudon County. Unusual but no miracle. Lee University is now a thriving institution with several thousand students and with many associated colleges and departments.

The college had been started in 1918 and was still rather small. We spent most of each summer for five years driving across the United States while recruiting students. I spent a lot of that time in the car as we traveled. I couldn't escape heated parental arguments. I read a lot and slept a lot. When reading, I could be anywhere in the world in any weather or under any conditions. This was my favorite way to escape reality.

When we first moved to Cleveland, I found my best friend, the Cleveland Public Library. I spent a lot of time there and checked out hundreds of books. I loved the orange biographies of famous Americans and must have read all two hundred of them. My favorite book was actually a two-volume set called *The Complete Works of Sherlock Holmes* by A.

Conan Doyle. Doyle actually was a medical doctor who had a lot of free time when he began his medical practice and wrote about the adventures, deductions, and observations of his detective Sherlock Holmes.

I enjoyed school and I attended the fifth through eighth grades at Arnold Memorial School. My favorite president was Abraham Lincoln and I even won a first-place ribbon in the fifth grade with this poem:

He was thin, awkward, big boned and strong
His face was homely, his hair was long
The cabin they built wasn't too tight
They kept a fire burning day and night
He used his axe to split a rail
And used his hat to carry the mail
In eighteen hundred sixty three
Lincoln set the Negroes free
As a president, Lincoln was good
He always listened and understood

All these facts were diligently retrieved from the *Encyclopedia Britannica*, my favorite encyclopedia. Winning the blue ribbon for first place and reading it for the school was one of my proudest moments in grade school.

We had an hour of music once a week and I learned many songs that I still remember: "The Battle Hymn of the Republic," "America the Beautiful," "La Cucaracha," "My Grandfather's Clock," "I've Been Working on the Railroad," "The Marine Hymn," our national anthem, and many others. In physical education, we learned how to square dance. I think this was my initial exposure to socialization with girls. Most of the Bible verses that I can now quote were learned in the one hour of Bible we had in our classroom every Friday afternoon. Thank God for the childhood ease of memorizing the beautiful poetry of Psalms and Proverbs, most of which I still remember and use. These included many life lessons also.

When I started eighth grade four months before my thirteenth birthday, I was 6 feet tall and weighed 185 pounds, made straight A's, and loved baseball. I was given a few nicknames including "Big Ox," maybe because we read about Paul Bunyan and Babe the Blue Ox but probably for my size and I must admit that I was somewhat—okay, maybe a lot—clumsy. My dad had always promised that if I got a whipping at school for any reason, I would get the same treatment at home. I remember several eighth graders were arguing, pushing, and shoving in the cafeteria lunch line and becoming quite rowdy. Several of us were pulled to the side by a large seventh grade teacher who used a reinforced Bolo paddle to give each of us five licks across our behinds. Because I knew I would get the same treatment at home, I kept it a secret and never mentioned this fact to my dad. I confided in my mom who willingly helped keep my secret.

I wanted to play baseball and be a catcher like Yogi Berra but I wasn't that good. I made up for it by reading everything I could about baseball and the New York Yankees. I enjoyed listening to the Yankees on the radio. I looked at the sports page every day and could read a box score. When Mickey Mantle came up in 1952 from the Kansas City Athletics, he became my hero. I still have a scrapbook that I kept about him during his run for Ruth's homerun record in 1957. I also watched Roger Maris hit sixty-one homeruns in 1961, which, because of eight extra games that season, gave him the record for homeruns. I even have a 1961 World Series ring with a beautiful one carat diamond, worn by Billy Gardner, a utility infielder for the Yankees. I was so worried that the ring could have been stolen that I wrote a letter to the baseball commissioner and found out the ring had been legally sold.

As an adult, I had heard of the Osborne Company which had created the original blueprints and velum drawings for Yankee Stadium. All were placed for sale. I now own over 100 of them along with a 1921 original blueprint of a stadium seat, which I have framed in my office, and an actual 1921 stadium seat taken from the stadium when it was renovated.

When CBS bought the Yankees from Colonel Rupert, it became the team most often shown on television. When color was added, it really brought out the beautiful green grass contrasted with the dark blue walls of the old Yankee Stadium. It was a good time in baseball to be a Yankee fan. They won a lot of World Series during those years. Mother knew nothing about baseball but at my insistence would keep track of each batter and write notes about what each player did while I was in school and couldn't watch. Her notes were hilarious but I appreciated her trying to help out. She even kept notes for me when Don Larsen pitched the only perfect game in World Series history in 1956. She never realized what had happened but her notes showed that no Brooklyn Dodger had ever reached first base.

I learned some good and some bad life lessons while watching the relationships my dad had with people at the college. He thought that anything that was not "nailed down" could be taken for his personal use. I had more Lee College notebooks and school supplies than I could ever have used. Bad. He included as his friends the maintenance men, cafeteria workers, dormitory monitors, secretaries, teachers, and professors. They kept him informed of everything that happened at the college. Good. Dad had an immense natural talent in music and could play many instruments "by ear." I saw him play the piano, saxophone, flute, trombone, and clarinet.

Dad brought his sister's husband to the college where he worked in the maintenance department. They actually lived on campus. I saw my first photograph of a naked woman in a nudist magazine I found in a desk drawer of an old house that the college owned. I never mentioned this to anyone. In fact I cut out one of the pictures and kept it in my billfold for a couple of years. I was always fearful that someone would find it. Another secret.

I mentioned earlier we traveled a lot in the summers. Once we went to Minot, North Dakota, where there was a small Church of God school, to recruit students for Lee College. We went across the border into Saskatchewan, Canada, to another school to recruit . All the kids wanted to be my friend and even bought me vanilla ice cream with peanut butter spun into it and hamburgers. I still love both. The kids said I talked with an accent. I thought the special treatment was great but I knew they were the ones who were talking funny.

Since I was so tall, I sat in the back of my classes during most of grade school. I could never see the chalkboard at the front of the class. One day after noticing me squinting and then coming up very close to the board at the end of the day to write down my homework assignment, my teacher suggested an eye exam. Since that initial exam, I have always worn glasses or contacts.

My first year in high school, Dad wouldn't let me go to the public high school but made me go to Lee Academy which was the high school associated with Lee College. I had new teachers and made a lot of new friends from all over the United States. The fad at that time was to peroxide the front part of your hair to make it blonde. It took what seemed like an eternity to convince my father to allow me to do this. My freshman picture in the annual confirmed the fact that he finally consented. One of my classmates was red headed and when he peroxided his hair it became pink. The only time I remember taking an IQ test was in the ninth grade- I did very well. My freshman history teacher was the person who administered that first IQ test. Once in his history class, I chewed a piece of paper in my mouth. We called it a "spit wad" and, using a rubber band, I held the missile between my front teeth. I launched it and hit my teacher in the middle of his forehead. I acted as if I didn't know what had happened but I think he knew. Only because my father was president of the college was I able to get away with this act of defiance and stupidity.

I began playing basketball at Lee Academy and enjoyed it. It was made more difficult by my wearing glasses and the fact that we had no protectors of any sort. I broke a couple of frames and even cut my eyebrow once. Dad was really upset and I was lectured about being careful and was threatened with punishment if I broke another pair. The next pair I broke was going to be a disaster for me. When it happened, my mom took me downtown at lunch and helped me get the glasses repaired. I don't have any idea how she paid for it but Dad never found out. Another secret. I may have even used some of the money I had made from selling *TV Guides* in our neighborhood.

Sometime later when I was in high school in Lenoir City, my mother lost her favorite sunglasses. They were dark blue plastic with metallic flakes in them. What really had happened was that Dad and I had found them broken and threw them away. However, I was instructed to not tell Mom. Many years later after Dad's death, mother and I talked about the incident but at the time it was a "secret."

Punishment was still a large part of my life. We attended church at one of the largest churches in the denomination, the North Cleveland Church of God. Dad still preached every Sunday night at the college while we were there. I would sit with Mother in the large auditorium with the student body and question her about many things my dad said. I never got any answers, but I always seemed to be able to figure out ways to get whippings.

I played a lot of board games because card games using a deck of cards or any games using cards were prohibited by church rules. I was great at Monopoly and won most games I played because I was banker and could cheat when counting the money. I always assumed that was acceptable if you didn't get caught.

Dad continued his education at the University of Chattanooga. I rarely saw him during daylight hours unless it was at church. He seemed to always be studying. I think the fact that he had a BA, was working on his master's degree, and valued his education, was rare for ministers in the Church of God at that time. I had already realized that since Dad was president of Lee College and I was a PK, or preacher's kid, I was treated with kid gloves. I believe it was Dad's education and continuing education that caused problems. I know it caused trouble for him with officials in the higher echelons of the church leadership. Many of these minister leaders were not university educated and/or had children at Lee College. Some were possibly jealous. The ones with children at Lee demanded their kids get special treatment when demerits or failing grades were given. You could get tossed out of school for grades or getting over 100 demerits. It eventually led to these men asking Dad to leave the college in 1957 and us moving to a small Church of God church in Lenoir City, Tennessee. Uncle Raymond, who was my mother's brother, had just pastored there. I never really understood my dad's demotion from college president to rural church pastor. Another secret.

During this period of time, I had a couple of interesting happenings. We were in Memphis, Tennessee, at the Claridge Hotel for an event called the General Assembly of the Worldwide Church of God. There was lots of preaching, beautiful singing, and politics. Almost like a political convention of sorts. Decisions were made to appoint state overseers, missionaries, and the general overseers of the entire church. Dad attended all of these and by being a minister, was a voting member. There was a lot of behind-the-scenes maneuvering and many appointments to churches, and then ministers trying to swap churches for their own priorities. Mom and I rarely saw Dad during the entire week. Most of the meetings were from early in the morning until late afternoon. Nights were filled with preaching and singing.

Most mornings Mom and I were free to sleep late and visit friends and family. One morning Mom had already gone downstairs to the lobby of the hotel to meet with some of her friends. There was not much to do in a small hotel room so, being bored and very inquisitive, I investigated almost everything. In one of the garbage cans in the bathroom, there was a white cardboard tube and a small white plunger that fit inside. I thought this was an unbelievable find and put it in my pocket as I rushed downstairs to be with my mother. On arriving, she was talking to three or four other women and I stood in front of her and excitedly showed her my new discovery. She immediately grabbed the device from my hand and quickly placed it in her purse. I was totally confused but not a word was uttered by my mother or her friends. Years later I found that the shiny white tube was a Tampax inserter and was taboo, at least for me. Another secret with no explanation.

During that same week of convention, Mom and I were walking down the street and "window shopping." We were almost back to the hotel when I noticed a crowd standing around a body crumpled on the sidewalk. Blood was everywhere. A man had picked that exact time to jump off the tenth floor of the hotel and had landed on the concrete. On his head. I broke through the crowd and got up close to the body to get an unobstructed view. That kind of incident really attracted me and I was not repulsed by it.

About ten years later, my father had obtained his Doctor of Education degree and at a similar Church of God convention he was elected by the pastors who were voting members to the executive committee of the Worldwide Church of God as the third Assistant General Overseer. He was never popular with some of the—in my opinion—uneducated elite ministers of the church. He was very popular with the local ministers and laypeople. He was either the first or second local minister to have been elected to the general executive committee of the church. The other overseers backhandedly rewarded my father by having him handle the care of widows, orphans, and missionaries and any problems they had. He made some futuristic changes in these departments which even eventually helped my aunt Odine. Dad advanced in leadership until he became the general overseer for the entire Church of God. Dad passed away in that position at fifty-one years of age—the same age his mother had passed away. I believed for years that I would follow the same pattern and die at fifty-one.

In Cleveland I never left home overnight for any reason unless it was for church camp. Even there, rules persisted. Most were for keeping the boys and girls separated. I learned that the swimming pool at church camp actually was two swimming pools. Boys swam on one side and girls swam on the other side. This meant that when families visited, the fathers and sons were on one side and mothers and daughters were on the other side. I believe, as many studies show, that separation increases desire. My vivid imagination could keep up with the girls especially since I was supposed to forget that they were swimming in the pool next to us.

On one occasion, a female cousin of mine returned home from church camp and told her mother, "I finally did it, but I washed my hands afterwards." My aunt was distraught and almost fainted. After several minutes of questioning, my cousin admitted that her indiscretion had been that she had held hands with a boy and broken one of many prohibitive rules. As in any situation, many of the rules were broken. At that time I was still in the stage of keeping the rules. I made my share of mistakes later and broke many rules. Mom and Dad must have found solace in Proverbs 22:6 that reads, "Train a child up in the way he should go: and when he is old, he will not depart from it."

I felt that Christmas and birthdays were supposed to be special and separated. Since my birthday was two days after Christmas and I usually received a limited number of gifts, I wanted to make my birthday just a little bit different from Christmas. I would tell my mother, "If you're going to take one of my Christmas gifts and give it to me on my birthday, could you at least take the Christmas wrapping paper off and put birthday wrapping paper on it?"

I must have asked constantly for three months before Christmas and my twelfth birthday for a three-speed bike to replace my old red-and-white Schwinn bike with wide white-walled tires. That was the only present I got for Christmas and my birthday that year. I learned a lot about asking for things from my heavenly father. Matthew 7:7–8 AMP says, "Ask and keep on asking and it will be given to you; seek and keep on seeking and you will find; knock and keep on knocking and the door will be opened to you. For everyone who keeps on asking receives, and he who keeps on seeking finds, and to him who keeps on knocking, it will be opened." Some prayer requests I thought I needed and some I just wanted. Over the years I have been impressed with both the answers to my prayers and the nonanswers. For many years I have kept a journal which includes asked, answered, and unanswered prayers. Amazing to look back over the years and ponder about what I have received and, just as importantly, what I have NOT received.

CHAPTER 6

We moved to Lenoir City in 1957 while I was fourteen and just before my second year of high school. Lenoir City was a town of about five thousand people and was twenty two miles southwest of Knoxville, Tennessee. Our church was on 6th Avenue and had approximately one hundred fifty members. Lenoir City High School was one block away from my home which was at the corner of 6th Avenue and B Street. There were no trailer parks or people of color in town. Most of the houses in my neighborhood were made of wood but a few of the newer ones were brick. The church had just built the new brick parsonage. There were still a few outhouses remaining at the back of some of the older houses.

It was just after we moved when my father asked me, "What do you want to be as an adult? A minister or a doctor?" I had watched and been present for a lot of what he had done over the years he had been a minister and how he was the first one to be called when people needed counseling, financial help from the church, or when sickness or death intervened. These calls were placed to our house even before a doctor or funeral director were called. I figured my dad knew me pretty well and which of those two professions I would choose. My response was, "Dad, that is no choice! I don't want to work as hard as you do. I'll be a doctor." I knew you had to be called by God to be a successful minister. Little did I know at that time and only realized at a much later date that there was an equal calling for me to become a doctor. If I'm not mistaken, I am either the first or among the first few to become a physician in the history of the Church of God. I have a feeling that everyone has a definite calling, whether it is manual labor, teacher, doctor, farmer, or secretary. I think that most parents should not be telling their children that they can become anything they want to become. Maybe they should be telling their children as Martin Luther King did, that whatever they want to become, they need to be the very best one possible. After I told Dad I would be a doctor, everything became centered around that decision.

Lenoir City was laid out with Main Street or Broadway being at the foot of a large hill. Main Street was where all the shopping, groceries, car lots, radio station, and post office were. And all of the avenues parallel to Main Street were numbered from 1st Avenue up to 5th Avenue at the top of the hill where the high school was located and then down the hill and back up another to 9th Avenue. Sixth Avenue was halfway down the back side of the hill and was where the 6th Avenue Church of God was located. Our house, which was again owned by the church, was located next to the church but faced B Street. All the streets perpendicular to Main Street were A, B, C, D, E, F, G, H, and I. So we lived at 701 B Street and everyone knew we lived at the corner of B Street and 6th Avenue. It was very easy for everyone to know exactly where everyone else in town lived.

I would get the kids in my neighborhood to catch rats for me. They would chase rats throughout the neighborhood and throw bricks at them and occasionally hit and kill one. Then it was brought to me. I would sit on the curb in front of our house at 701 B Street and dissect the rat using a kit my father still had from his college days. With blunt scissors and a dull scalpel, I was able to open the rats and dissect out intestines, heart, lungs, and diaphragm. Usually there was an audience of kids watching.

I did many projects for high school and for my own knowledge. One included taking blood samples from my dog's ear and blood from my finger. I smeared these blood samples on glass slides so I could examine them under a microscope. You could obviously see the difference between my blood cells and the blood cells of Dutchman, my cocker spaniel. I remember how one of my classmates and I would buy a cow's heart with help from the local butcher. We would take the heart into my friend's basement and dissect out the coronary blood vessels, atria and ventricles, and the valves separating them, the cords holding the valves in place, and the pulmonary veins as well. We spent many hours studying the anatomy of beef hearts.

Soon after I got to Lenoir City, I cut the top of my right hand on a rusty tin can lid. After traveling six miles to the hospital emergency room in Loudon, only a nurse was on call. She looked at my wound and said, "That's not so bad," and cleansed it with hydrogen peroxide. She used tape strips or "butterflies" to close the laceration. There was only one doctor in Lenoir City and he treated my father without charge because Dad was a minister. That included my mother and me until I got my first job. After I was employed, I was charged for my care.

Corporal punishment had become a regular part of my life. It seemed I was always in church. If other kids were rowdy I was usually in the middle of it and therefore got plenty of whippings. Once while we were in Lenoir City, my dad harshly called my name from the pulpit during the service. For once I was not involved in anything at all. That scared the other kids around me and they responded by being quiet, which was what Dad wanted to achieve, but it embarrassed me immensely.

On one occasion I had chased a neighborhood kid and caught him in a doorway in the basement of our house. For some reason I had pushed him up against the back of the door. I was drawing my fist back to hit him when my father called me and asked, "What are you doing?" I stopped in mid swing and replied to my father, "Nothing." I had learned that the definition of truth depended on a momentary feeling or period of time and not in actuality what was happening. I believe most of my behavior came from trying to avoid punishment or getting caught for the misbehavior. Punishment still consisted of Dad talking with me, praying with me, and then my getting whipped with his leather belt. No running around him because I was bigger than he was. I now had to lie across my bed.

As I grew up in age and size, punishment increased and many times I got bruises on my butt and upper legs. This became an embarrassment to me in high school where we wore shorts in physical education. Sometimes the bruises showed. I guess I rationalized that other kids laughed and kidded me because sometimes they came to school the same way.

The high school administrators had things figured out because they realized that many students were not going to college. Most would take vocational training, which consisted of auto mechanics, or shop which included carpentry. Some of us perpared for college. There was a limited number of jobs to be had in Lenoir City. Most people worked in Oak Ridge or Knoxville.

Many kids smoked between classes, and weekends included beer while in high school. I did neither because I was taught it was wrong and could cause many problems. But mostly I did neither because I feared my dad.

Dad believed that I should not attend any sport functions because of our religious affiliation and me being the preacher's kid. Although I played basketball my sophomore year of high school and we won the Tennessee State Basketball Championship in 1958, some members of the 6th Avenue Church of God were not happy with my involvement. That sophomore year was the only time I was able to participate in sports. As always, I remained interested in baseball. In October, I would sit next to the radiator in math class so I could ground my crystal radio and listen to the World Series.

Three of the players on our 1958 championship basketball team were 6 feet 7 inches tall or taller and all were over twenty years old. One went directly from high school to pitch for the Pittsburgh Pirates baseball team. The age limitations for high school attendance came later. I don't think you can attend high school now after age nineteen.

When I was fifteen years old, I dated a fourteen-year-old girl who was anxious to get married and have a family. I was supposed to be at basketball practice one afternoon but went by her house which was close to Memorial Auditorium where we practiced. She was the person who taught me about French kissing and we had actually swapped chewing gum on several occasions. As we were in the midst of getting physical, I could hear my father's voice telling me *If you ever get a girl pregnant, you are going to drop out of school, get married, start work, raise your family, and then I am going to kill you.* I hastily got up and left her house. I had walked about half a block when my father came over the top of the hill at 5th Avenue. I was immediately hauled home and with no questions asked, received the worst whipping of my life. The young girl found someone else and soon got married. I think she ended up with five or six kids.

Because of my father and our church rules, I couldn't go to movies or dance. I did attend the Junior Senior Prom with a girlfriend, who was a senior. I remember picking her up in a two-door 1949 Chevrolet and taking her to the prom at the Memorial Auditorium. I had previously spent most of the afternoon trying to figure out whether I should wear a necktie or not. This was a really tough decision for a junior in high school going to such an important event. I finally thought that it would be best to wear the tie and if no one else had one on, I would take it off and place it in my coat pocket. When we arrived at the Auditorium, I was trying desperately to be a gentleman. I walked around to her side of the car, opened the door, and held it open for her to get out. She looked at me and immediately covered her face and eyes. I thought, "What have I done wrong?" She said "Zip your pants." I was totally embarrassed, but I did zip my pants and we went inside. It was a long evening filled with a lot of conversation but I didn't dance—I didn't know how. But I knew the words to all the songs and still do.

She was the person with whom I had my one and only experience with premarital sex. This was considered a mortal sin and another secret that I have never mentioned until now. It was all premeditated. We knew her parents were not going to be at home. I knew that condoms were sold for a quarter per pack from a machine in the bathroom of the local ESSO gas station. I was nervous when she was one week "late" with her period. Since I didn't die just after the experience, I thought the earth would open up and swallow me whole. She was Baptist and we both worried for about one week before her period started. Approximately fifteen years later, she called and asked if she and her husband and two adopted children could come by our house in Chattanooga. It was a short visit, but she did manage to "secretly" tell me that she could never have any children of her own and we should never have worried.

Since there were so many things I couldn't do, it seemed the only option left was to excel in school. I was voted by my classmates for three superlatives that included most likely to succeed and most studious. Since I could only take one, I chose most likely to succeed.

We had a high school play my senior year called *The Curious Savage* by John Patrick and, naturally, I was chosen for the part of Dr. Emmet. I memorized the entire script after several practice sessions. I still use a picture of me in my white coat and the entire cast on stage as a wallpaper for my iPhone 6.

It was a common practice in Lenoir City for a person to be called by two names—their first name plus their middle name. Two of my friends were named Bobby Lynn, one of my best friends' name was Joe Paul, and another friend was named Mary Sue. All of us went to church together.

In fact Joe Paul, Vicky Lynn, and I began singing together in church and at other venues. We had a trio called The Crusaders. Joe Paul was amazing on the piano and still is. Due to our local popularity or the paucity of talent to come on their show, we were invited to sing on the Reverend and Mrs. J. Basil Mull Singing Convention of the Air. It was broadcast on Channel 6 WATE television, in Knoxville, Tennessee. This program was sponsored by one of the largest grocery store owners in East Tennessee, Cas Walker. He was lovingly called Cus' (short for cousin) Cas. He had a few years earlier helped Don and Phil Everly, better known as the Everly Brothers, get their singing career started on television. On Saturday afternoon we would drive to Knoxville to the TV studio. All performances were live and in person. We thought it was very cool to look at the TV cameras and wink at all the teenage girls who we were sure were watching us. We became quite popular in the area served by Channel 6.

Cas Walker suggested that if we would add a guitar to our group, we could become very popular and maybe even have the success that the Everly Brothers enjoyed. We did meet with a group of gospel singers called the Prophets who signed us to a contract. We even sang in concert with them once in Lenoir City. I personally knew I could not do anything to continue our singing career because of my commitment to become a doctor. So again I had a rather large decision to make: music vs. medicine. Right or wrong, I decided to pursue medicine and not a singing career. Miracle or coincidence?

Reverend Mull was almost blind and was a short man. Mrs. Mull was a much larger person than her husband. For the television show, she usually sat him on a pillow in the chair next to her to make him appear taller. Reverend Mull said he saw his wife across a large field while he was riding by on a Greyhound bus and became enthralled with her. We knew this could not be true as it appeared he could not see anyone more than five feet from him.

We were all present on one occasion when Reverend and Mrs. Mull were giving a nonscripted commercial for one of Cas Walker's grocery stores. Reverend Mull was saying that Cas had the freshest fruits and melons in Knoxville, Tennessee. He also commented that Cas had the largest selection of pecans, walnuts, and other nuts in his grocery stores by saying that Cas Walker had "the largest nuts in Knoxville" and Mrs. Mull joined in, saying, "Yes and I have seen them too!" This caused three teenage boys to actually roll on the floor laughing.

The local channel 6 also had live wrestling following the Mull's gospel singing show. We had just finished performing and before the trip back to Lenoir City, we would go to the small bathroom in the basement of the studio. It was there we saw all the "good guys" and "bad guys" wrestlers who were friends with each other and were deciding who would win or lose the bouts in the next hour. It was quite an eye-opening experience to realize that all the wrestling professionals were friends.

When my friend Joe Paul's father died at home, my dad was one of the first people to be called. I walked with him down to the end of the block on the opposite side of the street from where we lived. His father had vomited blood before he died and was lying in the hallway toward the bathroom. I always found those visits interesting and always tried to figure out what happened. I was not repulsed at all. My dad was frequently the first person called to go to a person's house when they were sick or dying or had passed away. I tried to always go with him. We always knelt in the living room with the family to pray for them. I have smelled many cane bottom chair seats in my life.

Within two weeks of turning eighteen, it was necessary to go to the county seat and register for the draft. In my opinion the whole purpose of the Army was to take young men and show them that in life there was someone besides their fathers who could tell them to do something and they had to do it with no questions asked. Maybe that's maturity and it's obvious that most young men mature much slower than most young women. When my four sons eventually made it to eighteen, our elected representatives in Washington had already decided to stop the draft and begin an all-volunteer Army. I think that a was a big mistake and believe all four of my sons would have matured much faster and better than they did if they had been made to spend two years in the Army. This was proven by my son Lincoln who attended and graduated from West Point.

When I went to the courthouse in Loudon, I was given a registration number. The first number was 40, which was the rank of Loudon County according to population of the counties in Tennessee, 57 for the population of Lenoir City, 42 for the year I was born, and 236 as an individual number. I went to Knoxville to the Army induction center for a physical examination. This included undressing and carrying around all your clothes in a wire basket. Along with thirty or forty other young men, I sat in line naked until they called us individually. After they found I was going to medical school, I was accompanied to the front of the line and had all my paperwork signed. They did not want to miss out on having a physician who would eventually serve in the Army. I distinctly remember the medical doctor who spoke to me and asked if I wanted to go through the usual physical exam or have him just sign the paperwork. Thank God, there were no hernia exams or rectal exams for me. Even though I had flatfeet with no arches and later discovered in medical school that I was color-blind, I would be acceptable as a physician in the Army. I spent many hours at the University of Tennessee in ROTC (Reserve Officer Training Corps) as a lieutenant and learned the basic fundamentals of marching, tearing down an M1 rifle, polishing my belt buckle, and spit-shining my shoes and brim of my hat. Demerits were obtained because of poorly polished belt buckles or shoes or improperly cleaned weapons and were worked off by hours of marching in uniform.

It turned out that when I graduated from medical school in 1967, the Vietnam crisis was at its very apex of activity. Because of the Berry Plan, I was told that all the names of eligible physicians would be randomly selected to immediately go in the Army, to go in the Army after one year of training as an intern, or to be allowed to finish the full four or five years of their training. I didn't have to enter the Army until 1972 after five years of surgical training. Miracle or coincidence?

My first job in Lenoir City was working for the mayor, Mr. Hamilton, who had a large farm on the outskirts of Lenoir City. Among other crops, he grew hay. We followed the tractor that pulled the hay baler. Each of the bales had to be thrown on the back of a flat wagon pulled by another tractor. After we piled the bales as high as possible, they were carried to the barn for storage in the upper portion of the barn. I learned very quickly that the twine holding the bales together could really tear up your hands and forearms. We had to pick up the bales by the twine to throw them on the flat trailer. This was hard hot work and none of us were told to, or had the sense to, wear a long-sleeved shirt and gloves.

I realized there must be something better to do than follow a hay baler. No matter how enjoyable the ride back to the barn on top of the wagon and hay bales was, it didn't last long enough. A conveyor belt took the bales up to the attic of the barn. We would ride the conveyer belt up to the top storage area of the barn when we could get away with it. Mr.

Hamilton also owned the small grocery store next to his house on 6th Avenue across the street in front of the church. He had all the necessities including essential groceries, candy, and carbonated drinks. I guess his was one of the original convenience stores. The Coca-Colas and Pepsi-Colas were called "dopes." I was always told that this was because the original fountain Cokes had cocaine in them. I guess the terminology came from that.

My next job was putting tobacco plants in the ground. It took three people to do this. The first person leaned over and with a premarked stick made a hole in the ground. The second person dropped in one tobacco plant while the third person merely stepped on the side of the hole in the dirt to close it around the plant. Hard, hot work again unless you were the third person. I realized there must be something better to do than plant tobacco.

Next I tried sales and I worked on commission at the Thomas Hill men's store. I was to sell pants, socks, belts, and shoes. It was very difficult to sell extra clothing articles to people who knew exactly what they needed (usually just underwear and socks) and had very little extra money to spend. I realized I was not a salesman.

My first real paying job was at the White Store, a local grocery store. I made 60 cents an hour and believed I was rich. I could not imagine making a penny for every minute I worked. Since I was relatively new to the town, the other workers still considered me an outsider and thought I was a city boy. Most of the businesses were closed on Sunday and there was an ordinance in town that no beer or wine could be sold in the grocery store at any time. We bagged groceries for customers and sometimes the bags seemed too small. I was asked to go to the back of the store for a "bag stretcher." I spent the next thirty minutes lying down waiting for the other bag boys to come get me. They finally figured I had some common sense. Most of the people who came into the grocery store asked that their groceries be placed in brown grocery bags but most people called them "pokes." The shopping carts were called "buggies." We rarely ever got tipped, usually only when an out-of-state person from much larger cities in the north or west visited our small town.

The assistant manager was called "Beans." I went along with him most evenings when he put money in the bank's night deposit box. The bank was right next door to the White Store. It had snowed most of one winter afternoon and coming back from the bank, we made snowballs. I launched a snowball right through the middle of the O in Store on the sign on the roof of the White Store. To my surprise the sign was made of canvas and the snowball had gone through it. Even though "Beans" was the assistant manager, no one ever made mention of the incident. Another secret in a rural town.

There was another city ordinance that required all black people who came in town to shop, even at the grocery store, to be out of town by sundown. I never saw any instance where this caused problems. Most of the blacks lived in "Buck Town" which was two miles away. We went there frequently to buy firecrackers and got there by walking down the railroad tracks. There were never any difficulties with us white boys being there; both we and the residents interacted well. I think most of the black kids were bussed to Sweetwater, Tennessee, to attend high school. I never understood why they didn't go to school with us. Now I know it was due to federal regulations regarding integration.

On one July 4th holiday, we had purchased firecrackers which were probably more dangerous then than now. My friend Bobby Lynn was driving a 1950 Ford that he had fixed up and worked on in auto mechanics class in high school. I had lighted an entire pack of firecrackers and flung them like a Frisbee toward his car. He was slow in rolling his window up and the entire pack of firecrackers exploded inside the car. Bobby Lynn and five others came streaking out of the car like rats deserting a sinking ship.

On Halloween that same year, I was with the same group of kids. We walked past the house of our high school principal. One of the guys had a brown paper bag full of his own poop. He sat the bag on the principal's front porch and lighted the paper with a cigarette lighter and then rang the doorbell. On coming out, our distinguished principal noticed the fire and stomped it out. He got a lot of poop on his shoes.

At my thirtieth-year high school reunion, none of us appeared to have changed much at all. I saw my classmate who had studied the anatomy of a cow's heart with me in the basement of his house. He became the owner of a recording studio in Nashville, Tennessee, with some big-name country music stars like Barbara Mandrell, Charlie Pride, and Ronnie Millsap recording there. He had even made his secretary Silvia a country music star. He attended our class reunion driving a Mercedes. The guy who was salutatorian in my class drove a Bunny Bread truck. Another classmate became a sheriff and one was an anesthesiologist. Another friend owned the local funeral home in Lenoir City and thanked me for helping him pass American history. I didn't remember helping him study but on further questioning found out that Bobby Lynn sat behind me in history and copied from my test paper and he had sat behind Bobby Lynn and copied from his test paper. I had helped two of my friends pass American history and never even realized it.

My dad was a conservative Democrat and voted for Adlai Stevenson both times he ran for president of the United States. He would not vote for a Catholic, John F. Kennedy, in 1960. My mother voted for Kennedy because she thought he was good-looking. I think my dad made a salary of close to $4000 my senior year in high school. I wanted to do better. I had already decided I was going to have seven children and be able to succeed with my thinking and my education. When I became a doctor, things would be great. I think I have maintained my father's conservative Democratic viewpoints but was attracted to Republican entrepreneurial ideas. My wife now enjoys college and professional football and picks her favorite teams by deciding which team has the best-looking quarterback.

I think my love of poetry came from singing songs in church. We didn't have a formal choir. Most of the time our choir was made up of church members who wanted to sing and would come up at the beginning of service and sit in the elevated seats facing the congregation. Most of the songs were new, very fast, uplifting, and promising for the future. However, there were several songs I remember vividly and was immensely frightened by them. I enjoyed the happier, faster songs that made my heart glad. I always figured on going to heaven, I just didn't want to go on the next bus. As a child I was very fearful of not being able to live a full, long, and exciting life before I was taken to heaven.

Elvis Presley was the king of rock 'n roll in 1957 when we moved to Lenoir City. Elvis made his debut on the Ed Sullivan show that year and I think that almost everyone in the nation watched. I had asked my father so many times that he finally relented and I missed Sunday night church in order to watch. It was a thrill to see Elvis, although they didn't show him from the waist down because of his vulgar "swiveling hips." I was almost as excited when I finally got to wear blue jeans on Sunday night rather than dress pants and white shirt.

Elvis was also memorable for many, but especially for me because I met him in person. A cousin and I waited outside Graceland. We both were there with our families while attending a Church of God General Assembly in Memphis. Having nothing to do during the day and before the services at night, we were able to go to the gates in front of his residence. We stood outside the gate for an hour or so before Elvis came out in the backseat of his black limousine. He was the first person I had ever seen with his shirt unbuttoned from the top with several heavy gold chains hanging down from his neck. When he saw us there, he had the car stop, shook hands with us, and spent about 30 minutes talking to us. During that time, a small elderly lady came up and brought him an apple pie. He smiled and said, "Just give it to one of my guards, please." Those guys must have eaten well. My cousin sent me a copy of her high school newspaper with a picture of her hands on the front page. Under the picture were the words, " These hands have touched Elvis."

Our church faced 6th Avenue. It was a brick building and there were approximately ten feet between the steps of the church and the curb of 6th Avenue. My first introduction to a Volkswagen was when three of my friends and I decided to lift a Volkswagen that was parked on the street in front of the church and place it front of the steps facing the church.

It was easy to lift and carry the car to its final position. Having no idea of the independent suspension of the rear wheels, we all were very upset and thought we had broken the rear axle because the rear tires angled toward each other when the car was suspended. You should have seen the look on the faces of people who came out of the church first. That was another well-kept secret.

Across the alley on the side of the church lived an eighty-five-year-old lady that we called Sister Rollins. She made some of the best fried apple pies I have ever eaten. She lived in a one-room tar paper-covered shack. Before she made pies, she cut her apples into slices and laid them on a 4-foot-by-4-foot sheet of plywood for them to dry naturally. Of course they drew multiple flies. She kept a yard stick with a piece of cheesecloth attached to it to swat the flies away from the apples. She sat in a rocking chair in front of her house and in between bouts of napping, she would wave the cheesecloth over the apples. I wonder if the occasional raisin in the pies was a fly. They still were the best fried apple pies ever.

As kids, most of us always preferred to play outside. The number of programs on television was limited and the best were on at night. Mom had "soaps" either on the radio or on daytime TV. Dad did not watch a lot of television. Most of the time Dad was studying for his Ed D at the University of Tennessee and I rarely saw him. In fact the only program I remember him watching was when the two of us would walk next door to Mr. Ellis' house and watch the *Friday Night Fights*-boxing sponsored by Gillette. I remember Rocky Marciano, who became the only heavy-weight champion in history to retire with a perfect record. I remember Jersey Joe Walcott. Archie Moore broke the record for knockouts as well as held the record for the oldest champion at age forty-eight. Ezzard Charles was a common name. Joe Lewis was finishing up his career. Floyd Patterson became the youngest heavyweight champion in history. I remember Cassius Clay in the 1960 Olympics waving a small American flag after a win. I became a boxing fan and had many heroes because of my dad's love of boxing.

Country conversation frequently used the term "fixing to." Later in life many people laughed when I used this phrase and asked what it meant. I believe it started in the Southeastern United States and was an attempt to explain how commerce was developed in communities. For example, in Tennessee there are ninety five counties and each has a county seat. In the early 1900's, people would gather their produce, chickens, eggs, and anything they had made like jellies, jams, cakes, and handmade furniture, and take them to the county seat. The pickup trucks were backed toward the courthouse all around the square. People would walk by on the sidewalks to buy or trade products. The term was used to explain how they were getting things ready, or "fixing to," take their products for sale or trade to the county seat. This still occurs in many counties in the Southeastern United States.

We played games like "kick the can." The intersection of two crossing streets was considered home base. One person was chosen to be the jailor and then everyone else ran away or went to hide. When someone was caught or found, they were brought back to the intersection which was called "the jail." If anyone was fast enough, he could run in and touch a "prisoner," then everyone else was released and the game started again. Many times we could not find one particular guy because he was "making out" with some girl or hidden in a dark area where we could never seem to find him.

We also played cork ball in the street. We had played a similar game in Cleveland, Tennessee, but used a round cork ball wrapped with Johnson & Johnson one-half inch white adhesive tape. We played with only two players, which was the most we could usually find to play. In Lenoir City we took a thermos bottle cork and used the same one-half inch white adhesive tape to wrap the cork lengthwise. This permitted the pitcher to get better spin on the ball. We then took a broom handle to use as a bat. With three players we were able to have a pitcher, catcher, and batter. With the cork ball being shaped as it was, it was easy to throw curves to the right or left and make the ball rise. The pitcher threw the ball underhanded. An open flat handed throw would cause the cork to drop and was considered an illegal pitch. If the batter swung and missed, and the catcher caught the missed pitch or strike, the batter was out. With each out, there was a rotation from pitcher to catcher, catcher to batter, and batter to pitcher. We hit singles, doubles, triples, and home runs. Each was delineated by a mailbox or telephone pole on the side of the street that the ball went past. If the hit stayed on the road, it was fair. If the cork ball was caught in the air as a fly either fair or foul, it was an out. We kept track of hits, errors, batting averages, and home runs. We spent many enjoyable hours playing cork ball. Statistics were kept in our heads, the greatest computers ever.

We also played touch football in the street which led to a permanent hand injury for me. I tried to catch a very low pass. It hit the ground and bounced up, hitting the very end of my right little finger. Nothing was broken but evidently a ligament complex at the middle joint of my right little finger was burst. As usual we were all afraid to report this to my parents as it might get all of us in trouble. Thank God, the injury caused my right little finger to be frozen in a functional position. My finger has not ever interfered with any of my surgeries. Miracle or coincidence?

There were also "submarine races" at the dam, built by the TVA (Tennessee Valley Authority), which backed up water to form Fort Loudon Lake. When you said you were going to the "submarine races" with a girlfriend, it meant you were "necking" or into "heavy petting" in your car parked there. We could always find our friends' cars but could never see inside due to the fogging of all the windows.

There was a smaller parking lot for observation of the locks. Many times we watched boats being taken through the locks from the lake to the lower river or from the river up to the higher lake.

Beneath the dam, water came through the turbines and fish were chopped up. This gave constant chum when the turbines were on. Some of the largest catfish, well over five feet in length, I have ever seen were pulled out below the dam.

In the summer we would go out to the lake to swim and cool off and float on old inner tubes. Always adventuresome, I attempted to go to the bottom of the lake to see how deep it was. The only way I could make it down was by slowly exhaling air from my lungs. When I got to the bottom, I mired up in two feet of mud and sludge. I immediately found out that I had let out almost all of my breath and could not float back to the surface. It was all I could do jerk my leg out of the mud and swim directly overhead or up to break the surface and gasp for much needed oxygen. I really thought I was going to drown. Coincidence or miracle?

The distance from where we turned off Main Street to the bridge leading to the dam was exactly a quarter of a mile. Another Bobby Lynn used to see what speed his father's 1955 Chevrolet could achieve before it hit the quarter mile mark. I think he was lucky to top out at 60 MPH.

There was also a Christmas parade each year downtown and the weather was almost always cold. People would line both sides of the street. Several of us were standing in a parking space just in front of an old 1949 Chevrolet. A woman was inside her car and to keep the heater on, the motor was left running. The car was in neutral. While leaning forward and revving up the motor to keep the heater going strong, she accidentally hit the gear lever on the steering column, and the car lurched forward. Four or five people were knocked down and were screaming under the car. Energized, four of us lifted the front end of the car. We were able to pull everyone out with only minor injuries.

One winter day there was enough snow for us to begin sledding. We had already tried using wide water skis to come down the two blocks from the top of 5th Avenue down the hill past our house on B Street. This did not work as well as we thought it would, so we started sledding. For those who had them, sleds were much faster than using a trash can lid or an upside down car hood as a way to come down the street or even steeper back alley. We never sledded down the long side of the hill toward town because it was five blocks straight down and through Main Street. There was a stoplight at B Street and Main Street. On one occasion a ten-year-old boy wanted to try the long route. He started at the top of 5th Avenue and picked up speed to the point he could not stop. The rest of us were standing at the top of the hill next to the high school. The traffic light on Main Street was green our way for a while but changed to red, allowing the traffic to begin through the intersection on Main Street. We were all yelling and screaming but the kid could not hear us. Or stop. An eighteen-wheeler started from the light and was in the intersection as the boy and sled went right under the trailer of the truck. He stopped unscathed about a block away. Coincidence or miracle?

One of the members in my father's church in Lenoir City was a used-car salesman. As a courtesy to our family, he loaned us a 1949 Chevrolet Sedan as a second car. I learned to drive using that car. It had first, second, and third gears along with reverse on the steering column. He had loaned us an earlier car, a 1948 Chevrolet, to use. It also had all four gears on the steering column. My mother embarrassed me on many occasions while learning to drive that car. As everyone who has driven a car with a clutch and gears knows, it takes a lot of coordination to push in the clutch, change gears, and slowly step on the gas to make the car start in a smooth manner. Mother could never seem to do this in a way that worked. She would make the car jump several times and then stop when she tried to start in first gear. Every time the car stalled, it was necessary for me to get out, raise the hood of the car, and pull an elbow joint back up, in order for the car to be started again. Even though she thought it was hilarious when she tried to get the car started in first gear, I would slink down in the seat next to her to prevent being noticed by my friends. She might have been laughing loudly, but it was very embarrassing to me.

After we moved to Lenoir City, Dad bought a 1957 Fairlane 500 Ford. It was black with a gold stripe like a checkmark along both sides of the car. My father liked the car but my mother did not and refused to drive it. Dad took the car back to the dealership within three days. He then decided to get a 1957 Oldsmobile 98. It was a beautiful two-toned blue car with a headlight dimmer on the dashboard, triple horns, overdrive, and a backseat that was almost big enough for me to lie down in. He paid for the car with cash—three $1000 bills. At that time I had never seen a $1000 bill. You could still get them from the bank then. He took the money from his savings account. I wish I had learned from observation or even better yet had my father teach me about saving. Soon after that I had all the credit cards and debt that I could tolerate.

There were a few opportunities for entertainment in town. There were always basketball goals in backyards. For more organized games, we went to Memorial Auditorium. Baseball could be played at the high school ballpark downtown. There was a small restaurant that had a tabletop bowling machine for a dime a game. The big attraction was a new device called a trampoline. One entrepreneur started a business which was new to us. Trampolines were placed over four rectangular pits dug into the ground. This was on a small corner lot at B Street and Main. For only a quarter, you could spend fifteen minutes bouncing. Some were coordinated well enough to try forward or backward flips. Most of us had never heard of or seen anything like this. On Sunday afternoons we could go to a farm about halfway to Knoxville to ride horses at $1 an hour or we could drive into Knoxville and play Putt Putt miniature golf at $1 a game. There was always swimming at the lake and if you knew anyone with a boat and outboard motor, there was water skiing. We bought 45 RPM records of pop music, which at that time was mostly country music, for 99 cents. I went to sleep almost every night with my record player softly playing a stack of records like the Platters "Smoke Gets in Your Eyes" or Frankie Valli and The Four Seasons singing "Sherry". My folks tolerated it well.

The biggest industry in Lenoir City was the Yale & Towne Lock and Key Manufacturing Company. They had a large parking lot which, during the winter, frequently was covered with ice. Most of us kids would go there to learn how to drive on slick and icy surfaces. We found that you could control the skid of a car by turning the wheels in the same direction as the car was skidding. I remember "winding out" the '49 Chevy in second gear by slapping the gear shift up into second gear while pushing the clutch in very quickly. The end result was that the clutch did not come back up and I had to drive the car home in second gear. Being embarrassed was not as bad as my fear of having to tell my father what happened. Dad's car salesman friend was very understanding and replaced the clutch.

The used car lot of Dad's friend was located on the south end of town as I remember. On one Thanksgiving Day, after advertising for several weeks on the radio and in the newspaper, he was going to give away live turkeys to people who came down to his lot to look at used cars. Joe Paul, Vicky, and I sang several songs at the event and then took several turkeys to the roof of his office building as he had instructed us. He thought we could throw them up in the air and have them fly toward the waiting crowd. We did as he asked but realized too late that most turkeys cannot fly. It caused a great commotion among the crowd on the ground. After a short chase, three or four of them caught a free live Thanksgiving turkey.

One of the earliest stories I heard concerning medical care was when my dad related a story about the used car salesman. He was a rather large man. Today he would have been called morbidly obese. He had complained of rectal pain for several days after eating a large meal of fried chicken and all the fixings. He went to a chiropractor who x-rayed his back and found that his spine was out of line. After adjustments and another week of pain, he decided to go to a medical doctor. The doctor did a rectal exam because of the pain and found the long portion of a chicken wishbone that had gone all the way through his intestines and become lodged in his rectum. Removing the bone relieved all his pain. This caused me not to trust chiropractors for a long time. Later, as a physician, I realized that one reason they were popular and helped people was because the chiropractors, as their name implies, place their hands on the patient during "adjustments," and always give their patients a diagnosis.

In later years I read many studies that showed that by sitting down when talking to your patients, you could get a better history and the patient would respond better to your care. The same studies show that touching a patient improves chances of healing and well-being. Other studies have used a double-blind technique where neither the physicians nor the patients were aware of which group they were in. One such study showed that one half of the patients in an intensive care unit were prayed for by a church that believed in prayer and healing, and the other half were not prayed for. The congregation of the church was not even in the same town as the hospital. The half that received prayer improved, recovered more quickly, and had a lower mortality rate than the half not prayed for.

The chief of police in Lenoir City was a 5 foot 2 inch tall man we called "Shorty." We would occasionally set fires in the intersections of the avenues and streets just so we could call the police. We wanted to get "Shorty" to come out to wherever we were, scream curses at us, and threaten to take us to jail. He usually came out.

In fact we had no jail but there was one in Loudon, the county seat. It was right next door to the bridge crossing the Tennessee River. On crossing the bridge, you could look into the jail cells and frequently prisoners would sit in the open windows and peer between the bars. We would yell, "What kind of bird can't fly? A jailbird, ha, ha, ha!"

Sex education was between zero and none. When I turned fifteen, my father gave me a book to read called *Into Manhood* (I still have it). It contained drawings of male and female genitalia with rather sterile descriptions of what took place during masturbation, the sex act, and surrounding issues. Of course I read the entire book several times. One Sunday afternoon our house was completely quiet. I thought my parents had gone visiting and I was looking for the sports page and comics of the Sunday paper. I walked through the house searching for the newspaper. When I got back to my parents' bedroom, which was in the back of the house, I opened the door. The sight that greeted me agreed with one description given in my book. I closed the door. It always amazed me that over the years both of my parents knew what had happened and what I observed momentarily, but nothing was ever said about that incident. Rather than a teaching moment, another secret was created.

Most of the sex education I received was in high school and was not as an official course but told by classmates and expounded upon in the streets. I was always amazed that one older classmate could use the "F" word five times correctly in one sentence, "What in the f...ing f... are you f...ing f...ers f...ing with?" I was taught that cussing was stupid but was not a mortal sin unless the Lord's name or God's name was used in vain. Once the same older teenager was holding forth his views on sex in front of Mr. Hamilton's small grocery store. There were four or five of us standing around listening. There was a twelve-year-old boy who was in the group. The teenager calmly stated that if a boy masturbated, he grew a wart in the palm of his hand with a long black hair growing in the middle of the wart. We all had a good laugh as the twelve-year-old quickly looked in the palm of his right hand. The only sexually-transmitted diseases that we knew about were syphilis and gonorrhea. Both of those logically could be prevented by using the condoms found in the bathrooms of the local gas stations.

I completed grades ten, eleven, and twelve at Lenoir City High School. I graduated third in my senior class of just over 100 students. I was the only student to have four years of language, four years of mathematics, and four years of science, including chemistry and physics. I ended up with four or five credits more than was needed for college admission. Typing was the only class I made a grade lower than an A (I got a B) in all of my years of high school. Typing and use of the keyboard prepared me well for medicine and the electronic medical records that I now use daily in the hospital and in my office.

After graduating from high school on Friday, I started to the University of Tennessee ten days later at seventeen years of age.

CHAPTER 7

When it came to college I had no choice. Dad pointed to Knoxville and said, "The University of Tennessee is that way...." I knew where the university was. Mom and I had gone there with Dad when he graduated with his Ed D degree in 1959. Dad was one of the few students to go through the master's and doctorate programs at the University of Tennessee with a straight A average. He knew it was cheaper living at home and commuting to the university than living there. In-state tuition was also much cheaper when I attended the University of Tennessee College of Medicine in Memphis later.

Dad also knew that I could not be tempted to socialize as much in college if I didn't live in Knoxville and stayed at home under his watchful eye. To accomplish this, he bought me a brand-new 1960 "split pea soup" green Volkswagen "bug." It had a 36 horsepower engine and would go up to 60 miles an hour downhill with a good tail wind. I tried to achieve this every afternoon coming down the hill outside Knoxville as I came home from college. He purchased the VW with cash and it cost $1800. The car got about fifty miles per gallon and gas was only 39 cents per gallon. The gas tank had a capacity of ten gallons and it usually lasted all week. I charged three other Lenoir City students who were attending UT 25 cents for each round trip to Knoxville, which bought my gas for the week. The car had a radio but no turn signals or gas gauge. I had to use hand signals for turning right, left, or slowing down. No gas gauge was a problem at first. It would appear the car was running out of gas. When you felt the sputtering, you would have to find the lever on the floor to the right side of the gas pedal. Using your foot you could turn the lever to access the reserve tank. You had one gallon of gas remaining and Volkswagen always advertised that you couldn't be further than fifty miles from a gas station. Other problems were the horn and the door handles. If the weather was freezing, the horn could stick and sound a continuous beep. That usually happened about 2:00 AM. I had to get up and handle the emergency. If the door handle was frozen, I would have to use hot water to thaw it to get inside and jerk on the horn to make it stop. Usually it took several tries to get the beeping stopped. The original tires lasted 120,000 miles. I used the car in medical school and eventually sold it with 150,000 miles on the odometer for $450, one fourth of the original price. My second car in medical school was my dad's old large 1964 Chevrolet Impala.

Student loans were either nonexistent or I had never heard of them. I had heard of "dad loans" (gifts) and used them as needed. I worked most of the time in college and medical school to keep from being indebted to anyone. I was told many times that I was never to be a borrower, only a lender. Polonius gave this advice to his son Laertes before he headed back to school: from Shakespeare's Hamlet. If I hadn't been in such a hurry, I would have majored in English. I always enjoyed English literature and poetry.

The University of Tennessee was only a little bit more difficult than high school. It was necessary for me to take a very heavy load in order to finish in two years. I enjoyed a course in genetics where we reproved the genetic facts that Gregor Mendel had produced with sweet pea plants. In a course of comparative anatomy, we dissected sharks, cats, and other animals. I took a chemistry course in the summer where we synthesized nylon. This really made me wonder how such information would be useful to me in my future in medicine. I also had time for courses in boxing, gymnastics, and one of the most important discoveries in my career, "how to find the library." Working with Physician Assistant students now, I find they know nothing about a library and believe all they need to know is on a smart phone. To complete my studies, I needed several hours of upper division courses. These included The Family and How to Build a Successful Marriage. I made an A in both courses but failed in life initially with both courses. That is until number three entered my life.

I think the two most interesting courses I took in preparation for medical school were Latin and Greek etymology. Both courses gave root meanings for words that came from each language. You can imagine how easy this made medical terminology. It also assisted me in knowing the definition of many words in English because of their origins in either Greek or Latin. I remember my mother helping me with the rote memorization of many root words. One stands out in my mind. Sarc is the root for flesh and is used in many medical terms eg. sarcoma (a fleshy tumor), sarcoid (flesh like), rhabdomyosarcoma (fleshy skeletal muscle tumor). I was barefooted, which was usual for me when inside the house, and was having a hard time remembering what the root sarc meant. My mother pronounced the root word and it sounded like "sock." I looked down at my bare foot and noticed my sock was flesh, so to speak. It was a memorable way to remember that "sarc" means flesh.

Mother was a real champion of mine and helped me do repetitive mundane things that brought good results over the long haul. I found out during the time of studying genetics that color blindness is passed down from grandfather to grandson through the mother's X chromosome which she received from her colorblind father. Mother received the colorblind X chromosome from her father which she passed down to me. My aunt Maudelle gave her colorblind X chromosome to her son Norman, my cousin. We both were colorblind because of our common grandfather. I don't think grandpa ever knew he was colorblind. Being colorblind had not affected me because whatever color I saw I had associated with the name of a color. I never even realized I was colorblind until my Med Lab course in medical school.

My grade average during my two years in college was 3.3 out of 4. This was not the kind of average I needed for medical school, but for carrying a heavy load of courses and finishing in two years, I guess it was not too bad. My advisor in college couldn't believe my schedule but allowed me to continue on the course of finishing in two years in order to attend med school. I was in a hurry because Dad couldn't continue supporting me forever and I couldn't work any harder. I had overheard a conversation at the Student Center between two of my professors. They had mentioned a young man who had just taken his Medical College Admissions Test test and even though his grades were not the best, he was a sure shot for medical school just from his score. I knew they were talking about me acing the MCAT test! Coincidence or miracle?

Just as Dad had pointed to the University of Tennessee in Knoxville and told me to go to college, there was no choice for medical school. Memphis was cheaper by being an in-state student. I met number one and medical school when I was nineteen years old.

CHAPTER 8

When I started medical school in September 1962 before my twentieth birthday, I had no debt. I remember how at that young age I had to appear before what I considered to be a group of old men, probably deans or professors, who actually made up the admission board of the University of Tennessee Medical School. I answered their questions about why I wanted to become a doctor. I never mentioned that Dad had given me the choice of being a minister or a doctor. I gave them my actual thoughts and answers which I am sure they thought were altruistic and "knight in shining armor" answers. Later both reasons became a real part of my life. When I was treated for codependency at Christmastime 1988, I was told that abandonment as a child and being a "knight in shining armor" for my patients and all those altruistic answers were my problems.

Attending medical school was an entirely different world for me. I thought medical school would be like high school and college. It was not. Mother wasn't there. I was away from home for the first time and had to take care of myself in all ways. I had to take care of my laundry instead of Mother doing it for me. I found a local laundry called "In by 9 dirty, out by 4:30." I had gone to high school and college with a grading system of letters and numbers. An A was 95 to 100, a B was 85 to 94, a C was 75 to 84, a D was 70 to 74, and an F was below 70. We were now on a pass/fail system and I had no idea where I stood or how I was doing in my medical school class. At the end of one year which included failing and repeating the third quarter of medical school, I received a telephone call at home. This was just after exams. I was told that I had failed out of medical school. Another secret that very few people knew until now. I had thought I could manage and had managed everything. I failed and my parents knew. This was September 1963.

At the time, I thought all was lost. For some reason I was allowed to meet with the dean of the Medical School. I don't remember exactly what happened but, after a long discussion, he said I could be readmitted to medical school in March of 1964. Miracle or coincidence?

One of the reasons I failed out of medical school was that I never found it necessary to fend for myself. Medical school was not the place to learn. I don't think I ever knew where the washing machine and dryer were at home. This was the first time away from home for me and someone taking care of my every need. Dad had written several of my English papers and short stories for me when I was in college.

A second reason was that when I came home between the second and third quarters of medical school, I ran a temperature between 104 and 106°. Not knowing what was wrong, my parents took me to Baptist Hospital in Knoxville, Tennessee. I was immediately admitted. Along with medication, I was packed in ice many times to bring my temperature back toward normal. The doctors thought I had leukemia or some viral process going on. Part of the workup included a rigid sigmoidoscopy. At that time there were no flexible sigmoidoscopes. The doctor used a rigid tube about three quarters of an inch in diameter and about twenty inches long. He used that scope to look at the last portion of my rectum and colon. I was placed in the knee/chest position on an examining table with my butt high in the air. The physician took the rigid sigmoidoscope and passed it the full length of my rectum and part of my sigmoid colon. It was very painful. No anesthesia was given. I was very uncomfortable when the physician performing the examination said, "I hear you're going to medical school. Sometime in the future you can tell your patients what a sigmoidoscopy is like." I turned my head sideways trying to get a good look at him and responded, "If I ever tell anybody how this feels, I'll never get to do one." By exclusion they finally diagnosed me as having mononucleosis, or "the kissing disease." I left the hospital early, against the doctor's advice, and even talked my parents into driving me back to medical school the next day. I was too weak to drive. Recovery usually required a three to six week period after being hospitalized for mononucleosis. I had lost approximately twenty pounds and was not functioning or thinking correctly.

A third reason I failed medical school was that I had entered a totally different world. People spoke a different language that I had never been exposed to and some had accents that were difficult to understand for a country boy. I had never seen a group of people who consumed so much alcohol. Many of them drank until they passed out. I was the designated driver because I didn't drink. I have never been drunk in my life. Fraternity guys had sex openly. I had a conversation with the fraternity president while he was covered with a blanket. Only as I was leaving did I notice a girl was lying under him. People used God's name in vain in routine conversation which I could never tolerate. They told lies and "borrowed" anything that they wanted which I considered stealing. I was naïve! Coming from a rural family and being a minister's son, I had led a very sheltered life. Many of the experiences in medical school were unbelievable to me. What you did had no effect on what you were trying to become. It shook my faith that so few medical students professed any faith at all. I was liked as a person, I think, because I had a habit of telling the truth to them even if it hurt. I complicated matters by flippantly telling classmates that I was from the mountains of Tennessee and had grown up on the side of a mountain and that was why one leg was shorter than the other. I told them I never had shoes to wear until I was twelve years old. I think some really believed this and considered me to be a "hick."

A fourth reason, I met number one. My dad had insisted that I attend a local Church of God while in medical school. I never had many dates in high school or college. I met number one in Memphis the first week I was there. She was attending the Church of God I visited. She was with a friend and both were going to the Baptist Nursing School in Memphis and both were starting their first year. The nurses' dormitory was adjacent to the library at the University of Tennessee medical school. Number one had been raised in the Baptist Church. We were attracted and immediately started dating. Her family had multiple secrets.

Maybe that was the initial attraction. She was from a small town in Arkansas. Her mother had six children. The oldest sister had been born to a father she never knew growing up and was already out of the house. The last four children had been born to her mother and a man who number one considered to be her father. Both parents raised the last four children plus number one. Another man had passed through Arkansas and after a brief liaison with her mother created number one. This was a secret in the family that no one was ever told. Number one discovered this secret one day while looking at a family photo album. She noticed a picture of her mother and a man she didn't recognize. After asking her mother who the short bald headed man was in the picture that she found, she was told, "That's your father." She thought maybe she favored the man. Her mother reluctantly told her what happened. Number one was loved by her mother and family but could not be fully accepted by the stepfather who raised her as his own. There were no difficulties in the family until the stepfather died and completely left number one out of his will. It always amazes me how money changes family thinking. Her family never gave her an equal share of their inheritance.

We were fast and furious with our dating and I believe it was the beginning of the undermining of my grades in medical school. I was young and dumb. I remember an episode once when I brought number one back from a date for her 9:00 PM curfew to the nursing dorm and my golf type shirt was inside out. I got a lot of kidding about that when the other nursing students were returning at the same time and noticed my shirt. It was only later that night that I realized what was wrong. In dating, I think I was looking for someone to take care of me. Dad always told me that if I was going to have sex, I had to get married. I believed

74

him. After I failed out of medical school in September 1963, I returned to Lenoir City, Tennessee, where my dad was still pastoring. Number one came up later and we were married in the latter part of December 1963 by my father.

I had to go to work to support us while we lived with my parents in Lenoir City. My father accompanied me to the University of Tennessee Memorial Research Center and Hospital to look for work and asked me, "What job do you want to apply for?" All I knew about hospitals was indicated by my answer, "Well, I guess I could be an orderly." He replied, "Why don't you ask about work in the lab?" I didn't even know where the lab was but when the woman in charge of the lab and the other ladies in the lab found that I was going to medical school, I was hired. They all took me under their wings and taught me how to work in a laboratory. I did venipunctures, learned how to run all the machines including the old Van Slyke CO2 machine, how to do complete blood counts, how to do a urinalysis, how to use pipettes, how to do spinal tap cell counts, and how to run the blood bank. I remember working many hours and also found that the third shift—from 11:00 at night until 7:00 in the morning—was my favorite to work. That shift permitted me to take my time, learn the machinery, and get good results from the tests that I ran.

While in charge of the blood bank, I considered it easy to draw blood with a large gauge needle, especially if the patients were young. On one occasion a seventeen-year-old young man came to give blood for his sister who was having surgery in the hospital. He said, "I will do anything for my little sister." I was able to get a 16-gauge needle in his arm for withdrawal of the pint of blood. He was very stoic and said he didn't even feel the needle going into his vein. However, when he fell to the floor and blood was pouring out of his arm, I realized he had fainted. I had to quickly take off the tourniquet around his arm, remove the needle, stop the flow of blood, and clean up the mess. I learned that most people will say anything and wondered if they could be believed in times of stress.

The University of Tennessee was also noted at that time for the beginnings of Dr. Bill Bass' "Body Farm" which was located adjacent to the hospital. I thought it was a fascinating place even though I was unable to see the research done there. Many people boycotted the Body Farm and marched around the fenced-in area and protested by carrying signs decrying the research done on decaying bodies lying outside in all types of weather conditions. At times the odors were unbelievable.

I learned to sleep whenever I got the chance. Coming home after I got off work at 7:00 AM and going to sleep caused no problems. It came in handy many times in medical school and during my surgical training. I learned to do all my work in the laboratory by on-the-job training with help from many people who thought they saw a lot more potential in me than I thought I had. I spent three months working in the lab at the University of Tennessee in Knoxville but again, I was in a hurry to get back to medical school.

CHAPTER 9

Number one and I returned to Memphis in March 1964 for me to start medical school again. Dad tried to help us buy a small trailer to live in while I was attending medical school. Being 6 feet 5 inches tall, I could hardly stand up straight in the shower of the trailers we looked at. We eventually rented half of an elderly lady's house for the first several months and shared the one bathroom in her house. Later we were able to rent an upstairs garage apartment adjacent to a large old mansion that was closer to medical school. After that we moved to an apartment complex called "fertile acres" because many of my medical school classmates who lived there started their families. The apartments would shake when a train rolled past in the afternoons and early mornings. My first daughter was born in April 1965 while we lived there. Soon after there was a miscarriage (another secret), followed by my second child and first son being born in May 1967 just before I graduated. Number one worked as a telephone reservationist for American Airlines.

Medical school was different this time around for several reasons. Professors had given up the pass/fail system of grading and gone back to the original numbers and letters grading. My second time through anatomy was a totally different experience because I repeated the same course but not the same mistakes. Knowing what to expect helped. The first day I raced to the smallest covered human body in the anatomy lab. As in life, there are fat and thin bodies. I wanted the thinnest and least greasy cadaver to dissect. I finished anatomy with the highest grade in class. That 88 grade got me an A. We lost about one third of our original one hundred classmates by their failure of gross anatomy. My partner failed anatomy. Across the table from me was a dentist who had tired of his dental practice and was now trying medical school. His partner failed anatomy. Neither of our partners showed up in class about half the way through the dissection of our cadaver. My friend and I had the entire body to ourselves. He taught me how to pull teeth, at least from a cadaver. Gross anatomy was an unusual experience because it was necessary to splay each anatomical part before we dissected it. Being a voracious reader it was interesting to remember that in Germany years earlier, Hitler had used human skin to make lampshades.

My anatomy professor was a PhD by the name of Dr. Harry Wilcox. Because a third of our class failed, he was nicknamed "Hatchett Harry." He was a brilliant man and understood human anatomy better than most surgeons I have ever met. He had an unbelievable amount of knowledge and it was amazing to see how he used his hands and instruments to show us anatomy. It seemed at times he could dissect nerves, arteries, and other anatomy by using only his thumbnail. He and we did not use gloves or surgical masks during our dissections. I helped in his research lab at times and found out that he was the "surgeon" at the Memphis Zoo. In fact he was doing research with a certain large male monkey in his lab. He had found the sex control center in the monkey's brain and ablated it. The male monkey became extremely "energized" and created quite a problem just with himself. A situation had occurred on the "monkey island" at the zoo. The island was surrounded by a 20-foot wide moat and outside the moat was a 15-foot high wall. The island had become a matriarchal society and the females would kill all the males placed there. Due to the lack of male monkeys, the population was decreasing. Only when Dr. Wilcox put his "super male" on the island did things get back to normal. The population boomed.

Most of the bodies we used in anatomy were stacked and stored in a

5 by 7-foot tank of formaldehyde before being placed in our lab for dissection. The soaked bodies reeked of formaldehyde.

We never noticed the smell while working in the anatomy lab. But in our last year of medical school, we could tell when the freshmen entered the cafeteria from the smell of formaldehyde that lingered around them. I'm sure that during our tenure in gross anatomy, we had smelled the same as the freshman did. It was very difficult to get the smell of formaldehyde off our hands and from underneath our fingernails, but it caused no problems for us while we ate lunch in the student center.

Occasionally there was an exception to the no-mask-or-gloves rule. A young man who wore both gloves and a surgical mask during dissection of his cadaver showed up at the beginning of anatomy classes. He acted strangely and stated that he was "allergic to formaldehyde." When I did an internship and residency at Baroness Erlanger Hospital in Chattanooga, Tennessee, I met him again. As an intern I was rotating in psychiatry. I noticed him in the "lockdown" unit of the psychiatric ward as a patient and almost did not recognize him. He had severe mental problems secondary to being forced to attend medical school by his father who was an MD.

I thoroughly enjoyed my class in anatomy. It was basic knowledge required for becoming a good general surgeon. Most people don't understand why and think I'm crazy, but I'm donating my body to the University of Tennessee for use in the anatomy lab to help beginning students learn human anatomy. The school has a program for physician donors and at my size, I'm sure I will be a good specimen. One of my pet peeves from anatomy lab and from my background with Latin etymology in college is the pronunciation of the word "dissect." Most people incorrectly pronounce dissect as if it rhymes with bisect, which means to cut into two usually equal parts. The word actually comes from the Latin root *secare*—to cut—and the prefix *dis*—apart. The word means to cut apart, not to cut in two parts.

We were a diverse group of medical students. We had a black male student who had been in the Air Force, two dentists, five or six women who were nurses, and several Jewish young men from colleges located in the northeastern United States. Most of the Jewish young men had fathers who were doctors. They added a lot of interesting background noise to our class. They would get medication from their fathers called "black beauties" or "bennies" and keep the drugs for themselves. These were amphetamines or weight loss medication which were used to stay awake at night to study. They were later pulled off the market. At that same time, samples of Ritalin were sent to medical students and I'm sure practicing physicians as well. They were considered innocuous. Ritalin is frequently used now in children with ADHD, but at that time we used them to stay awake longer to study for exams.

There were collections of old examinations called "test research," which were exams obtained from previous students and usually kept in fraternity house files. These were excellent guidelines for studying and we always hoped that some of the questions would be repeated on our exams. Some students found a cache of exams that none of the rest of us had and kept them just for their own use. They did very well on the next exam by studying the old exams. However, when the rest of the class found that these exams were used and the rest of us didn't know about them, the entire class had a meeting. Those classmates were persuaded to share information as we all did. Our unity made them realize that we were all in medical school together. If anyone got material that could possibly be helpful in studying, we would share with everyone. Most of the fraternities kept such "test research" and we became very good at sharing. Some of us even studied with classmates who lived at different fraternity houses.

I will never forget one of the medical students who came from Knoxville. His dad was a math professor at the university. He had a voice that cracked almost as if he were going through puberty. Sometimes his speech was hilarious. He did not do well in medical school but I think eventually became a family physician. He thoroughly enjoyed participating in intramural sports, especially softball. When he failed out of medical school, he was told he could return in three months. He decided that he would come back the next year only if he could return just before softball season began. We were studying one night at the fraternity house. The softball star was sitting in front of the TV set and several of us were sitting behind him. He put his forefinger in one side of his nose and came out with a large mucous concretion. Someone said, "Don't flip that booger" and he stopped. Not knowing what to do, he replied, "I'm not," and wiped it on his pants.

Anatomy lasted the first six months of our first year in school and some students actually saved small body parts of our cadavers. We were warned not to do this. The bones of the middle ear (the malleus, incus, and stapes) are very small. Many of the students saved these bones as well as patellas (kneecaps). After we finished dissecting the body, all the parts were gathered and were either sent back to a funeral home for family burial or sent to a potter's field in Memphis.

We had a class note-taking system. This was before tape recorders or other portable recording devices. Some of us did better in certain classes than others and would be the ones to take notes in the courses in which they excelled. They were responsible for getting a set of notes together, typing them, and getting them out to the rest of the class for studying. Believe it or not even with the varying shades of blue ink, we got most of the material that was presented to us written down and printed by mimeograph. Some rather raunchy and perverted jokes were inserted within the notes. You could always see one particular female student blush when she got to the jokes as she read the class notes.

At the beginning of school, we had a pathology rotation and took autopsy call. One of my three team partners had a noticeable shaking of his hands but if he did anything purposefully, the tremor stopped. He eventually ended up becoming a general surgeon and practicing 35 miles away from me in rural Tennessee. We assisted with many autopsies and rotated the chore of disemboweling the autopsy victims. No one liked to do this. It was necessary to open the entire intestinal tract with scissors and then clean out what was there and check for any unusual contents.

We had some utterly amazing and unusual professors in medical school. I will never forget the pathology professor who wore very thick glasses and was blind without them. He told us at the beginning of the year that we had to wear our white coats while in class. No matter if the pathology auditorium was hot or cold, we had to keep our coats on. One student had taken off his coat and placed it over the back of the seat in front of him. The professor spent five minutes trying to get the attention of what he thought was a student when he was really talking to an empty seat with a coat draped over the back of it.

One professor in histology had an extracurricular session or group called the "Smoke Benders." It was after classes in the evenings. He would present slides which included unbelievable artwork and architecture demonstrating pornographic scenes. I may have been the only one in class that was amazed at this. I only attended one of these sessions because I thought it was a waste of time and it actually offended me. However, I did find out some of his cold, hard facts about grading. There were two exams during the entire semester. I made an 84 or a C on the first exam and an 85 or B on the second exam giving me an 84.5 grade average which he determined was a C. He stated that he did not curve his grades and I should be happy with the highest C in class. I argued that I should have the lowest B in class and not be happy with the highest C given. I believe he recognized that I did not attend his extracurricular sessions. I got a C in the class.

In an anatomy lecture lab, we had to identify carpal bones that the professor would roll across a lab table at the front of the class. We were to write down the name of the bone before it fell from the end of the table. This was part of our final exam.

We studied many nights in the lab until the wee hours of the next morning. About two o'clock in the morning, a fellow student was sitting on a high stool beside his cadaver. He was from Nashville and attended Vanderbilt University. I think his father was a doctor. He yelled at the top of his voice, "Turn off the lights! Turn off the lights!" Someone reached up and switched off the lights for the entire lab. We were all sitting in the darkness. All of a sudden, he pulled his legs up and passed gas through his rectum. Using a match next to the seat of his pants, a fart became a yellow blaze approximately a foot high. That was the first time in my life I had ever seen a fart lighted. But not the last.

When we entered the last six weeks of anatomy, a younger professor from Czechoslovakia replaced Dr. Wilcox and finished the course with us as instructor. It was obvious that he was a force to be reckoned with. I had the highest grade in anatomy and was asked to come to his office. Earlier that day, I had talked to a graduate student who knew this new professor well. He told me secretly not to accept any offer of a final grade other than the one I had actually made on the exam. Not knowing what to look forward to, I entered the doctor's office. He offered me a grade of 93. I told him that was OK, I would just take whatever I made on the exam because I wanted to "play by the rules." After some pressuring he finally admitted that I had made a 96, the highest grade in class. Although the first six months learning human body was quite a chore, the knowledge obtained made my future in surgery look very promising.

In biochemistry we had an elderly professor who was unbelievably eccentric. He used a small bowl that held slips of paper with each of our names written on them. He drew names and the first name drawn was relieved of all duties or question answering that day except for changing the slides that the professor had prepared to be projected on the front screen. Any student's name drawn after that had to answer the next question asked. He would also make a big deal of either placing a large check or making a large X by each name on his score card of grades. Due to his exaggerated motions, it was obvious if the answer was right or wrong. Tinker toy type models of all the essential amino acids were hung from the ceiling. We had to look at the models and name them for one exam. He also graded papers by placing a checkmark on the front of each exam. He did not write either a number or letter grade. One of my classmates was obsessive-compulsive and asked how he could tell what grade he had made on the exam. The professor told him that the grade depended on the length of the tail of the checkmark. That student spent the next twenty four hours trying to measure the length of the tail of the every checkmark on our exam papers to try to figure out this professor's grading system. One classmate did so poorly on an exam that the professor told him his paper was down in his basement office, hidden there, and he must hunt for it. It was eventually found behind a picture on the professor's wall. The student complained that he had no idea what his grade was on the exam because it had a large +/- . The professor said he couldn't decide whether the student had failed or passed the exam.

The same professor was honed in on our powers of observation. He was trying to coordinate some of the basic science of biochemistry with the clinical findings in diabetes mellitus. He discussed in detail how if the kidneys were presented a high level of sugar in the blood, some sugar would spill over into the urine. He made quite a show of holding up a glass beaker of urine and stating that you could taste the sugar in the urine. I watched as he dipped his right forefinger in the urine and quickly placed his right middle finger in his mouth to demonstrate this. As a country boy I learned to be very observant at an early age. I think most of my class actually tasted the urine and agreed that it tasted sweet. I mimicked what I had seen my professor do and placed my right forefinger in the urine and then my middle finger in my mouth, and quickly agreed with him that it was possible to the taste the sugar in the urine. He likewise was very observant and gave me a knowing smile.

A professor in neurophysiology drew on the chalk board with colored chalk. He would use both hands when drawing. He could draw cross-sections of the spinal cord and nerve bundles with both hands. It was unbelievable to me that someone could do all this while lecturing at the same time.

For those of us in medical school who had to work to pay for our education, some students went to the local blood bank and sold a pint of blood for $15. Others were brave or crazy enough to give a sperm specimen for the same amount of money at the sperm bank. It was not uncommon for elevator doors to be opened on the first floor of buildings by pulling them apart while the elevator was on an upper floor. While one student held the doors open, another student jumped down one level to the elevator floor. Many times coins and even dollar bills were found there. That was crazy! The elevators were never disabled and could have come down at any minute. If that had ever happened, the student would have been trapped under the elevator.

During my second year of medical school, I discovered I was colorblind. We were in medical labs and were looking at slides of early red blood cell forms called *prorubricytes*. The nucleus and nucleoli were different shades of purple. I could not see the difference in these two colors and could not delineate the nucleus from the nucleoli. My instructor took me aside and asked me to look at a Japanese color chart for determining color blindness. This consisted of looking at colored dots in a circle and seeing the number in the circle. I usually could not see a number or could see only one of a pair of numbers. I failed miserably! After she knew I was colorblind, she gave me a lot of extra one-on-one attention. The color blindness was never a problem for me and never has caused any problems later in surgery. I still don't understand why some colors such as red and green cause no problems, but I have such difficulties with grays and purples.

During most lunchtimes there was a mad rush to the Student Center. There was a pinball machine in the basement that most of us became quite adept at playing, especially those of us interested in surgery. I guess it must have been the hand-eye coordination that caused the attraction. If we could ever find four card players, we played bridge. Sometimes these games carried over into the early hours of the afternoon and some 1:00 PM classes were even missed. However, the note takers were always there for us and even though we missed the class, we had our class notes to review for exams. It also led to situations that only medical students would think of and carry out. One bright sunny afternoon we left the Student Center and were late for out next lecture. We had just gotten our head mirrors (which are no longer seen except occasionally in an otorhinolaryngologist's office). They were used to reflect a light placed behind the patient. The mirror was concave and had a hole in the middle of it. You could look into a person's ears, eyes, or throat with the reflected light. That day we passed a group of nursing students. We fell into a single line and quickly placed our mirrors over our eyes to direct the bright sunlight into the nurses' eyes. Crazy.

I remember going to the state fair in Memphis and making a friend of a black giant who was over 8 feet tall. I spent over an hour talking to him about his medical condition. He was happy to have someone who understood why he had developed as he did. He had an anterior pituitary tumor which caused him to not only grow tall but after his bones fused, the tumor caused the diameter of all his long bones to increase. He had been born in New Orleans at Charity Hospital and was studied extensively after he outgrew the rest of the kids in his neighborhood. After many attempts to improve his condition, he made his living by traveling with the circus and appearing at state fairs. His fingers were so large you could drop a half dollar through the ring that was on the ring finger of his left hand. Years later when my youngest daughter and I were watching WWF wrestling on Satellite TV in Tennessee, we watched another pituitary giant who was one of her favorite wrestlers–Andre the Giant. He was over 7 feet tall and weighed close to 400 pounds. The general consensus was that he could not be lifted off the wrestling mat and body slammed. We saw Hulk Hogan lift him above his head on one occasion but when Andre shook his massive body, he fell on top of Hulk Hogan. Wonder how many people knew of the brittleness of Andre's bones and realized that if he had been body slammed, many of his bones would have been broken. It took me back to the time in Knoxville when I saw how the community of wrestlers worked together. Sort of reminded me how an elderly friend of mine thought that wrestling was real and men walking on the moon was fake.

Halfway through medical school, I was able to start work at Methodist Hospital in Memphis as an extern. This was an opportunity to make extra money while attending medical school and to begin using some of the skills learned in a course we had just finished—Physical Diagnosis. In order to admit a patient to the hospital, the attending physicians were required to complete a history and physical. They rarely did. I was paid two dollars for every history and physical (H & P) I completed. The supply was unending or so it seemed. It was very boring work but gave me an opportunity to make some extra money. I got to use many of the techniques I had learned at UT Hospital in Knoxville. I spent many hours giving Aminophylline very slowly intravenously through a small gauge needle usually placed in the veins of the hand or forearm. This medicine caused the patient a lot of pain where it was injected but it brought relief for their breathing almost immediately.

I had been taught to do a complete history and a complete physical. I had learned that most patients knew a lot about what was wrong with them and if I listened they would help with their own diagnosis. Talking to the patient sometimes required speaking in another language not just literally but figuratively. Many times I had to use the words that they understood but were not included in our medical jargon. Syphilis was frequently called "bad blood" and "gonorrhea" was called "clap." Along that same line, "low blood" was anemia or having a low hemoglobin, and "high blood" was hypertension. While obtaining a history from one particular female, I asked about "low blood" and she replied, "No." I asked about "high blood" and again she replied, "No." Then I asked specifically about the possibility of her having any sexually transmitted diseases. I asked her if she had ever had "bad blood" and she said," No." When I got to "clap," she thought for almost an entire minute and finally stated, "Well, I got stabbed in the chest one time and I got a clap lung." In her mind she associated her previous "collapsed lung" with having a sexually transmitted disease. It really meant that the stab wound to her chest had caused her lung to collapse. We found many other tests and names of medicine caused difficulty. A VDRL (which stood for Venereal Disease Research Laboratory) was a test we ordered for syphilis; Warfarin (Wisconsin Alumni Research Foundation) is a medication that thins the blood; and the drug Premarin (which stands for PREgnant MARe's urINe) is a female hormone replacement. Relating to a surgical history or physical, "fibroids" of the uterus were called "fireballs." Spinal meningitis was called "smiling mighty Jesus." All the exotic and rare diseases were usually easy to remember. Our professor always said, "When you hear hoofbeats, think of horses not zebras."

Many of the patients we saw in medicine clinic were elderly and had venous insufficiency ulcers on one or both of their lower extremities. These ulcers were very difficult to heal. One afternoon in clinic, I noticed that an elderly gentleman had very clean ulcers on his legs which were healing well. I asked him what his secret was for caring for his legs. He explained, "I leave my legs uncovered at home until the flies 'blow' them. Then I wrap them with newspaper (the printing ink used in newspapers usually made the paper sterile) until I come to the clinic to be checked." I looked more closely at the ulcers on both of his lower extremities and saw something moving. Sure enough there were maggots in the ulcers eating up all the necrotic tissue. I had heard about them but never seen them in a wound. The ulcers were very clean. Most of my classmates had never seen these small one-half-inch long wriggling creatures. Especially the students from New York City. I told them these were housefly larvae. They did not believe me. When I placed several of the larvae in a glass Mason jar and kept them there until they became flies, they accused me of removing the maggots and replacing them with flies. Even today there are medical maggots that can be obtained from medical supply houses. Fifty years later here in Florida, I still see maggots cleaning wounds especially in diabetic patients who have venous ulcers on their lower legs.

I received my first emergency or "stat" call which came on the overhead paging system while I was an extern in Methodist Hospital. I was in the bathroom at the time but hurried to answer my page, a call to start an IV in the emergency room. Although the operators could call you overhead at Methodist Hospital and at Erlanger Hospital in Chattanooga during the day, different systems were used at night. By using a lighted system in each hallway, numbers were flashed. That meant the doctor whose number was displayed was to call the operator for messages. This kept hospitals quiet for the patients after visiting hours and at night.

I also had my first introduction to physicians in private practice. There were twin older doctors with the same last name of course. They were call Dr. A and Dr. B. I first met Dr. B in surgery when he was doing a hemorrhoidectomy and singing "Jesus has been good to me, doo dah, doo dah." This was done to the tune of Stephen Foster's song "Camptown Ladies Sing This Song." I was to assist him in surgery and thought I was in the wrong place at the wrong time. It was almost sacrilegious to me. I had another opportunity in my last year medical school to meet identical twins who were both physicians. The first one came to our class and gave a lecture on Pediatrics. Later the next week his brother, who we thought was the same physician, came in and gave a lecture on Gerontology or the other end of the spectrum of life.

While I worked at Methodist Hospital as an extern, I met one of the largest physicians I have ever seen. He was 6 feet 8 inches tall and weighed over three hundred fifty pounds. He was one of the most mild-mannered gentlemen I have ever met. When he asked his patient to move from a stretcher to the delivery table just before the birth of her child and she had difficulties, he could just pick her up and move her to the bed with no assistance. I never saw him get upset or mad about any situation. After all those late night and early morning deliveries, I decided that most babies were conceived and born at night. I enjoyed obstetrics but surgery called.

I also met a senior resident in surgery who eventually became a plastic surgeon. He made unbelievable scenery for a model train layout that was kept in the resident's lounge. Using plaster cast material and chicken-wire mesh, he made beautiful hills, tunnels, mountains, and cities. All were painted in great detail. He was a fantastic artist. In later years I collected United States revenue stamps and heard that he was commissioned to do a painting of ducks for the United States Fish and Wildlife Service hunting permit duck stamp series.

A memorable and wacky intern at Methodist Hospital by the name of "Mad" Marvin was loud and boisterous. He had interviewed in several rural hospitals for work. He had arrived at one small town drunk and actually ran into a gas pump and knocked it over with his Corvette. He got out of any trouble by promising the rural sheriff that he was coming back to that town to practice medicine.

It was also at Methodist Hospital and during my rotations at the other hospitals in Memphis that I found out that common sense is not very common. Many fellow students, interns, and residents couldn't "come in out of the rain" even though they were quite intelligent or book smart. I assisted one professor who had written a textbook and was considered a world expert on stomach surgery. I think he held the world's record for being slow. I held the world's record of wishing I were somewhere else during his surgeries. He was brilliant but should have gone into teaching full time. Over the years I have seen it proven that the smartest surgeons weren't necessarily the best surgeons. Question: What do you call the guy who graduated last in his medical school class? Answer: Doctor

Baptist Hospital in Memphis was at one time one of the largest hospitals in the world with 2,100 beds. I was making rounds with a thoracic surgeon there on one of the cardiovascular floors. We saw several Catholic nuns who were nurses and were dressed in their habits. The surgeon would drop behind a garbage container and pretend to hide and say, "Spooks."

In the last year and a half of medical school we had clinical rotations including obstetrics, gynecology, and surgery. I delivered forty-two babies during my obstetrics rotation. I had a three hundred pound female come to the OB department when I was a student. After checking her abdomen, listening to her complaints, and doing a pelvic exam, I was able to tell her that she was ready to deliver a baby. "I can't be pregnant," she stated. "I've never been exposed to a man." I shook my head and replied, "Maybe not, but you're going to deliver a child very soon." After a few moments she said even louder, "But I've never been with a man." Again I responded, "You must have been with someone to get pregnant." After quite a lengthy pause she responded, "Well, I does sleep with my sister and her husband and I might have got splashed on." Another patient told me, "I haven't demonstrated in three months and I'm afraid I'm stagnant."

When we delivered babies in the delivery suite as students, one person gave anesthesia which consisted of oxygen and nitrous oxide while the other student delivered the baby. I had a classmate we called Herbert "Norman the Neck" Bunchman. He was delivering a baby boy while I was giving anesthesia to the mother. I asked her what she was going to name her child. She said she had no idea. I told her that her doctor's name was Herbert Bunchman. She thought that was a great name. Somewhere, maybe in Memphis, there is a fifty-year-old man with the name of Herbert Bunchman Jones.

One of my classmates was called "Bluto" because of his resemblance to Popeye the Sailor Man's nemesis. We had a picture of him being delivered out of a dirty linen chute with the use of Piper obstetrical forceps.

It was always hilarious to listen to the names that pregnant women came up with. One lady thought the nurses had already named her child "female" so she left that on her daughter's birth certificate (pronounced fe-mah-lee). Another patient was being wheeled into the OB department where she noticed a sign above her head over the door that warned "no smoking." When her son was born she named him Nosmo because her last name was King. Earlier in Cleveland, Tennessee, I knew a gentleman by the name of Mr. Pigg and believe it or not his first daughter was named Ima and a second daughter was named Ura. Unbelievable! In Jamestown I actually had a patient whose last name was Dover and his parents had named him Ben.

We could always tell young women who came in pregnant and were ready to deliver their first baby. They were called primaparas. We shortened this to "primips." They usually came in with their hair rolled up in pink curlers. They seemed to scream all the time between abdominal contractions. We also called them "squirrels" because they were usually extremely agitated and jumpy. They usually would yell, while trying to breathe through their mouths and not push down, "O, Lordy Jesus, help me now!"

One of the delivery room windows faced Baptist Hospital and many times it was so hot in the delivery suite room that the window was left open. There was no screen and the breeze through the window was refreshing. On several occasions moths would fly into the room and on one occasion a flying insect dove into an episiotomy wound. One early morning, a Catholic nun who was also an intern in the OB/GYN department had just delivered a baby with anencephaly. She seemed to be more interested in taking care of the baby, who could not possibly live, than she was of taking care of the mother who was actively bleeding. As students several of us stepped in to take care of the mother and saved her life.

We had organized our OB work each night. The person in charge was called the "rod." His assistant was called the "co-rod." Most of the black patients called the student in charge a "coordinator" but pronounced it "co-rod-inator." If you delivered a patient in bed before you got to the delivery room or "precipitated" a patient, you were charged 25 cents. This went into a "popcorn fund," and we always had plenty of money for popcorn.

I had a patient who came in during her last month of pregnancy with twins. Many times these multiparous ladies or "multips" delivered early and very easily. Of course I precipitated or delivered the babies in her bed before we could get to the delivery room. Since these were her seventeenth and eighteenth children, her uterus was very lax. We massaged her uterus after delivery but when we sent her down one floor to the OB inpatient ward, none of the nursing staff palpated or stimulated her uterus to contract. By the next morning her uterus had filled with blood and she died.

Most of the patients we saw in medical school were a reflection of the population in Memphis in the mid-1960s. The black population made up most of the indigent patients we took care of and we learned medicine while doing this. They got excellent care and were seen more times by medical students, interns and residents, and attending doctors than anyone in hospitals today. It seems as if everyone in medicine today is looking at their computer and not their patients.

In the OB/GYN clinic, we saw follow-up patients six weeks after delivery. My obsessive-compulsive classmate decided to use his own birth control system. He was upset that many of our patients seemed to get pregnant on their way home from the hospital and could actually not have a period for several years due to their frequent pregnancies. When women came in for their six-week checkup which included a pelvic exam, he would slip an IUD in their uterus and never tell them. He never mentioned this to anyone but told us about it on our next rotation. None of us approved but were too scared to report it. Another secret.

We had a call room in obstetrics and surgery that was similar to every call room I remember during medical school, my training in surgery, in the Army, and all of the hospitals I've ever been in.

All these rooms were totally devoid of any stimuli. There were no windows. There was no way of telling whether it was raining or snowing, daytime or nighttime, or about anything going on outside. I think that the person who designed these interior rooms knew exactly what they were doing. When the lights were turned off, the room was entirely dark and quiet except when the phone rang. I guess that's the reason I can go to sleep almost anywhere now, but my best sleep is in total darkness.

My first year in private practice, I returned to Memphis for a philatelic show. I was on a tight budget and decided that instead of going to a motel, I would try to spend the night at the hospital in a call room for surgery. After asking a nurse in the emergency room where the surgery resident's call room was, she gave me directions. I slept in surgical scrubs and the next morning went to breakfast in the cafeteria. I asked the cashier if the surgery residents could still sign their name on the receipt to get free meals. She nodded and I signed "Mickey Mouse." My entire overnight stay and meal were covered. I believe that you could probably travel across the entire United States doing the same sort of thing in most hospitals. If you stop by the hospital administrator's office and get a business card, the entire trip becomes tax deductible.

It was in the John Gaylor building that most of the outpatient subspecialty clinics were located. Patients could never find the correct clinic, e.g. urology, medicine, surgery, orthopedics, or OB/GYN, and no one could tell them exactly how to get there. Instead of answering the same questions over and over and no one really understanding the directions given, different colored stripes were painted on the floor. Each colored stripe directed patients to the correct elevator. The same color was placed beside the elevator floor numbers to select the correct floor. When the patient got out of the elevator, they could follow the same colored stripe to the correct clinic for their appointment. Simple, well-thought-out solution.

On our psychiatric rotation, we were all seated in an auditorium. The professor would bring in a patient and interview him in front of the class to give us an example of a certain diagnosis. A gentleman was rolled to the front of our class in a wheelchair. He introduced himself as Jesus Christ. The psychiatrist in charge was going to pursue a line of questioning to make the patient appear incompetent and give his real identity. He smiled at the man and said, "If you're Jesus Christ, perform a miracle." There was a loud murmuring throughout the entire class. The man quickly came out of the wheelchair and jumped on top of the examining table and screamed, "Quiet!" It became so quiet in the auditorium you could've heard a pin drop. The man turned to the psychiatrist and said, "That's a miracle!" Makes you think that some of the patients knew exactly what they were doing.

We also had a patient who was almost catatonic. She would only respond to a sound, like the jingling of keys on a keyring. She would give rhyming words or a long string of words that all rhymed like ring, king, ding, sing, ping. She crawled on the floor beneath the conference table and went over to where one of my classmates was sitting and started untying his shoes. At last, the instructor asked what she was doing. She responded, "Untying his shoes." Again it makes you wonder about some of the psychiatric diagnoses. The one physician in my class who went into psychiatry was fittingly named Dr. Fink.

I was told this story about the founder of Orkin Exterminating Company. Who knows if it is true or not? "Otto the Orkin man" was in the psychiatric unit in the basement of the John Gaylor building. His family was attempting to "put him away" because of accusations of eccentricity and dementia. He escaped the unit but without a stitch of clothing. He was running down the street naked when the police noticed him and after placing him in the patrol car asked who he was. He responded, "I'm Otto the Orkin man." They immediately took him to the psychiatric unit because they thought he was crazy.

Halfway through my final year in medical school, I became a suture student. The job ran from 7:00 PM until midnight and paid $3 an hour and all I could eat at a midnight meal. They probably lost money on that deal. I had never done any suturing of lacerations. But considering the fact that I was an aspiring surgeon, I thought I could do anything. The intern on call took me into a large room and briefly showed me how to suture an uncomplicated wound. I had read about the techniques but had never sewn up a laceration on a real live person. The emergency room was busy and the intern left me alone.

At that moment I looked up and saw about twenty patients waiting to have their lacerations sewn up by the new doctor—me, the medical student. I was anxious to get started and try out all different types of stitches and different sizes of sutures I had read about but never used. The intern brought in an obviously drunk society-type older woman. Her pink party gown was stained with blood from her nose. She had fallen, hit something, and had a one-inch laceration across the bridge of her nose. She looked at the young intern and then at me. She slurred, "I'm not having some damn intern sew up my nose." Without missing a beat, the intern quickly responded, "I'm not suturing your nose, ma'am. Dr. Carroll is." She turned toward me and said, "Are you an intern?" "No, ma'am," I replied. So she lay down on the examining table and became the first person on whom I had ever sutured a facial laceration. I often wondered how she reacted when she sobered up and a week later got her sutures removed.

After beginning work as a suture student, I spent a lot of time observing other situations in the emergency room which is now called Elvis Presley Memorial Emergency Room and Trauma Center. There was an actual jail cell or retaining cell present there in the ER. As I walked in one evening, a female patient inside the cell asked me, "Would you like to f..k my p....y?." I found out later she had actually inserted straight razors into her vagina. She then went out to Millington Naval Base which was just north of Memphis. She would have sexual relations with sailors causing them to have multiple cuts and scrapes on certain parts of their anatomy. Can you imagine the effect on a young naïve minister's son when events like this happened? Shock is probably the best word to describe it.

On another occasion I observed a young boy who had an arrow through his right temple with the feathers visible along the right side of his head and the point of the arrow visible and sticking out of the left side of his head. At first I thought he had one of the old trick arrows that went over the top of his head, making it appear that the arrow went all the way through. Upon further examination, the arrow was real and went directly through his skull at his temples. He was awake and alert when he was taken to surgery. The arrow was removed under a controlled situation and had only clipped off his pineal gland (an appendage just below his brain) but caused no other damage. He did well postoperatively.

Another time in the emergency room a man came in with his penis shredded. A few minutes later his female partner came in with a fractured skull. She had evidently had a seizure while performing oral sex on him. To distract and disengage her, he had hit her in the head with a Coca-Cola bottle.

Surgery was my last rotation and my favorite. I was able to spend a lot of time with the chairman of the surgery department, Dr. Lou Britt, who had me scrub on all his private surgical cases. I remember coming in early one morning after he called me at home. He cursed me out, asked me why at 2:00 AM I was asleep and not studying, and asked me to report immediately to the hospital for a surgical case. I learned the distinction that night between phlegmasia alba dolens (a swollen white leg due to arterial compression secondary to extensive deep vein thrombosis) and phlegmasia cerulea dolens (which indicates a severely swollen, cyanotic and blue, discolored leg secondary to deep vein thrombosis with possible limb loss). I will never forget the totality of that long night.

Most mornings in surgery started with 6:00 AM rounds on our own patients, followed by rounds with the residents at 7:00 AM. The attending surgeons made rounds about 7:15, and then we went to surgery by 7:45. I once scrubbed with a cardiovascular surgeon who was called the "Jolly Green Giant" not because he was jolly but because he dressed in green scrubs and was over 6 feet tall. He had a patient who was brought to surgery for mitral valve stenosis which would require opening the man's chest or performing a thoracotomy. He would then do a finger fracture of the mitral valve. I had recently received a Jaegar-LeCoultre alarm watch as a gift from my father. The watch had been placed in the pocket of my scrubs and the alarm went off. The surgeon looked around and asked where the sound was coming from. I was too afraid to answer. Thankfully the alarm soon ran down. A fourth-year surgical resident who later came to Chattanooga, Tennessee, was first assisting in the finger fracture of the mitral valve. The Jolly Green Giant asked if he would like to feel the fractured valve. The surgical resident acting as second assistant was asked next. Both took their turns. He then very condescendingly asked if I, the lowly medical student, would like to feel. OF COURSE! He held a Satinsky (vascular) clamp which was around the auricle of the left atrium of the heart above the mitral valve and opened it while I slipped my finger in the patient's heart while it was beating and felt the fractured valve. I was thrilled! I had placed my finger in a beating human heart!

One morning before we made rounds with our attending surgeon, I noticed a high-backed wooden wheelchair sitting on our surgical floor. The patient in the chair was held in a sitting position by several straps and was unresponsive. I asked the nurse if this was one of our patients. No one admitted knowing anything about the patient. The chief neurosurgical resident who later came to Chattanooga as a practicing neurosurgeon had the explanation. The patient had had a stroke a week earlier. And as an emergency, a craniotomy had been carried out, leaving the patient in a vegetative state. The attending neurosurgeon had not seen the patient initially and every time he came to make rounds with the residents, the nurses would move the patient down to our surgical floor so he would not see the patient and ask the residents questions about him.

The chairman of surgery who gave our didactic lectures no longer did surgery but was chief of surgery at John Gaston Hospital. For years he had done many general surgical procedures but was now semiretired. He would have the residents over to his house for a monthly "party." He always said there was beer in the refrigerator for those who enjoyed it. He usually kept two beers in the refrigerator. The residents never touched them, knowing he did not approve of any type of drinking.

Every Wednesday afternoon, we had a lecture by Dr. Wilson. We called it "prayer meeting" because we all sat there and prayed that he would not call us to the front of the class and ask questions. He had the reputation of making the surgery residents who presented cases and us medical students look ignorant. He had a penchant for not liking abbreviations. One chief surgery resident made a presentation and inadvertently used the term SSKI (an abbreviation for saturated solution of potassium iodide), which was used in thyroid patients. The resident was "dressed down" in front of the class and made to look very small. He remembered that later when I practiced surgery with him in Chattanooga, but did not like me to mention it. Dr. Wilson called me in front of the class on one occasion. When he started asking me questions about appendicitis, I thought I had it made and would stay out of trouble. Dr. Wilson had to be over seventy years of age. I was doing well with his questioning until he asked me the difficulties in diagnosing appendicitis. I very quickly responded that the extremities of age, the very young and the very old were the most difficult cases to diagnose. I gave a sigh of relief until he asked me, "And Dr. Carroll, what do you consider to be old?" I was trapped. I responded, "Much older than you are, Dr. Wilson." He did not laugh but the entire class guffawed.

I remember an incident in the surgeon's lounge at Baptist Hospital while waiting for a case to get started. As I walked in, I was greeted by a world-famous orthopedic surgeon who was over ninety years old and standing there absolutely naked except for his shoes and socks. He evidently was no longer capable of doing anything but minor surgery. But anytime he got the chance, he would come to the surgical lounge before surgery, remove his clothes, and if anyone came in who he didn't know, he would introduce himself to them. That morning I was there he knew that he had never met me. When he appeared in front of me, he asked my name, extended his hand, shook hands with me, and said "I'm very glad to meet you!" He turned around and sat down in one of the lounge chairs. No one said anything about his nudity.

About 65 of our original class of 100 graduated. One person was returning to the Army as a doctor (where he later was given the choice of being a doctor or staying in the Army but not both), one was going back to the Air Force as a doctor, and the rest of us spent the next two weeks finalizing our plans as to where we were going for internship and residency programs in our chosen field of medicine. Some of the larger institutions had internships and residency positions filled by a "matching program." Most of us had plans to go to areas where we would like to be in private practice. I chose the Baroness Erlanger Hospital in Chattanooga, Tennessee, because it was in east Tennessee and I wanted to practice in the area. There were four positions open for surgical training there. Erlanger was a 750 bed Hospital with an associated Children's Hospital approximately two miles away.

I had approximately three weeks to pack and move number one and two young children back to East Tennessee. This was a lot of responsibility for a twenty-four-year-old medical school graduate. My father was an assistant general overseer in the Church of God and lived in Cleveland, Tennessee, approximately thirty miles from Chattanooga. Dad and Mom lived in a Church of God parsonage that was very close to the house we had lived in previously in Cleveland. I moved my family into my dad and mother's home in Cleveland and lived there for several months after I started my internship in Chattanooga. I commuted to Chattanooga on a daily basis. With my father's help I was able to obtain my first piece of real estate. It was a three-bedroom, two-bathroom, 1800 square foot house with an unfinished basement on an acre lot. It cost $18,500.

CHAPTER 10

We had maybe thirty interns and residents in training in the various subspecialties at Baroness Erlanger Hospital. Each of the interns made $500 per month the first two years and $600 per month for the remainder of their training. We also got two sets of "whites"—short white coat and white pants. The pants had buttons (not zippers), and we wore white shirts with no tie. It was obvious that everyone could distinguish us from the "regular doctors."

Doctors fresh out of medical school were accepted at Erlanger Hospital as rotating interns because we spent three months rotating on predetermined (although chosen by us) rotations at the hospital. I chose three months on medicine, three months in the emergency room, three months in surgery, one month in psychiatry, and then two additional months on surgery. I spent most of the time on the other services looking for surgical procedures to do, for example thoracenteses, paracenteses, starting IVs, and performing liver biopsies. I would stick a needle in anything.

During that first year three of us new interns were coming out of the hospital to go across the street to the residents' quarters when an elderly man fell to the ground. He appeared to be having a heart attack. Later we found out that this was the same "frequent flyer" patient who came in the emergency room and fought for the "asthma chair." That chair got you seen very quickly if you complained of asthma. You could "cut" line in front of many other waiting patients. All three of us had learned basic CPR. One of the interns from Georgia saw the man fall. He immediately ran over and began mouth-to-mouth resuscitation. We watched as he vomited after each time he gave a mouth-to-mouth breath. An older nurse walked by the action and recognized the man. She sternly called, "Claude, get up from there!" He realized he had been caught and immediately got up and walked away. We were amazed that some patients did not tell the truth, especially those seeking pain medication or those trying to be noticed for some other reason. We were taught to believe our patients.

It was also during that first year of internship that one of the other interns from Georgia and I worked as employees for a local family practitioner. He was recovering from a heart attack and was limited as to what he could do in his office. We worked under his direction in his office for $5 an hour and did all sorts of minor surgery such as removing skin tags, lesions of the skin, and sebaceous cysts. We watched as the physician managed his practice. Drug companies sent him samples of medication such as antibiotics which were new and very expensive. Many different types of medication were kept in the doctor's office and dispensed to his patients. Even Valium was considered innocuous and samples were sent to him in the mail. He and his nurse dipped Q-tips in alcohol and scrubbed off the drug company name from capsules. They were then sold to his patients at quite a profit. I guess this could be considered our first exposure to a private practice and the financial considerations in a doctor's office.

Even in 1967 $500 per month was not a lot of money to support a family of four. Residents and interns were allowed to work extra in the emergency room and they were paid $2 per hour for a 12-hour shift— from 7:00 PM at night until 7:00 AM the next morning. The emergency room was busy enough that sleep was usually not possible during the shift. We could only work if we were not on call for our training. The hospital depended on us. None of the private doctors wanted to work in the emergency room for a 12-hour shift at night. My second year at the hospital in my first-year surgical residency, I was elected as president of the interns and residents. That included orthopedic, surgical, ophthalmologic, and medical residents and interns. It was difficult to work all day and then come to the emergency room at 7:00 at night and be awake and work until 7:00 the next morning when your training started again. We were on call for our surgical training every third night. I was asked by the interns and residents to talk to the CEO of Erlanger about a raise in pay. They asked me to propose a raise to $4 per hour for the 12-hour shift in the emergency room. I met with the CEO and he was adamant. No! The interns and residents met again and decided to go on strike. Getting one hundred percent of any group of doctors to agree on anything is like herding cats. We had all agreed to stand together. I went back to the CEO and again asked for $4 an hour. I told him we were going to go on strike and not work in the emergency room if we did not get the raise. He understood that working in the emergency room would not interfere with our regular duties. Again, he refused. As an aside, I mentioned that I could possibly avert the strike and get the residents and interns to agree to an increase to $3 dollars an hour. But again he refused. We all went on strike, refusing to work the extra shifts in the emergency room. It fell back on the private doctors to work. This lasted for less than one week. Most of the private practicing physicians sided with us. They told the CEO to give us anything we wanted because they refused to cover the ER. The CEO called me back to his office and asked if we could settle on $6 per hour. This continued good care to the emergency room patients but allowed us to make a better living for the time given up on our off-duty hours.

For the five years I spent in surgical training, we kept the surgical indigent or poor patients on a large ward on the third floor of Erlanger Hospital. One of the best assets we had were the nurses, many of whom were African-American. Things were a lot different at that time. They all dressed in starched white uniforms and wore starched caps. When the interns or residents walked up to the nurses station, they always stood and responded, "Doctor, can I help you in any way?" It was a joy to work with nurses who sincerely respected you and were intent on trying to help both doctors and patients. The best nurses were on the first and second shift. It was not an uncommon thing to find that the nurse on the night shift, who was usually less interested and caring, had written a note on the chart of a really sick patient, who had died during their shift, stating, "Patient was found dead in the bed."

I will never forget working with one of the best, Mrs. Harvey, when a patient who had cirrhosis and esophageal varices started vomiting up massive amounts of blood. We were trying to put in a Blakemore Sengstaken tube to prevent esophageal bleeding and empty the stomach of blood. A basinful of the vomited blood was sitting on the bedside table. Mrs. Harvey was helping me put in this large tube and getting it properly connected. The patient fought with us the entire time. While trying to restrain the patient, he kicked the basin of blood which covered both her and her starched white uniform. She never complained or stopped working. When we got the tube placed correctly, she excused herself and put on a set of surgical scrubs and never once complained about the incident.

One of my favorite nurses was about my size. Her name was Dolly Starr. She was always happy, smiling, and wanting to help. We had a patient come in with priapism, or a sustained erection. This condition can be very painful for the patient. We had tented the bedsheet over the top of his engorged organ. While we were making rounds we discussed surgery and how we could drain his penis by attaching a vein from his leg to one of the corpora of his penis in an attempt to salvage it. Dolly sidled up to me and whispered in my ear, "Dr. Carroll, give me ten minutes alone with him." I smiled and replied, "Dolly, that wouldn't help him at all." And she responded quickly, "Hell, you ain't going to help him either." Sobering words of wisdom.

The very first day I walked into surgery, an older nurse ran down the hall and jumped into my arms. She said, "Welcome to surgery." I was flabbergasted and wondered again if I was in the right place and had made the correct decision on becoming a surgeon. This was totally different from anything I had ever experienced. I always figured that it must be a reaction to the intenseness of many surgical situations and necessity for some people to be totally removed from the seriousness of their work. That nurse later married an anesthesiologist who had five kids. She was divorced with four kids and after their marriage they had two more kids. Thank God for His protection.

I got to do my very first gallbladder removal (cholecystectomy) in a very unusual way. One of my favorite doctors was a private attending Jewish physician. He was great teacher and believed in teaching by letting you do surgery and followed the old adage of "See one, do one, teach one." He always operated in room number five of the surgical suite at Erlanger Hospital. A first-year surgery resident and I as an intern were scheduled to help Dr. Reisman perform a cholecystectomy. We were standing outside his room with the patient lying on the stretcher. He walked up in front of me, the patient, and the first-year surgery resident and asked, "Which one of you birds is going to do this gallbladder?" The first-year surgery resident without hesitating or flinching replied, "Leonard is. He's never done one before." The patient's eyes became as big as saucers! However, I did my first gallbladder. Believe it or not, the patient survived.

Dr. Reisman's daughter-in-law was a nurse in the intensive care unit. She knew the intensity of our training and how many hours we spent working. If someone passed away in intensive care during the night, she would wait and call us early the next morning before rounds so we could get a good night's sleep before coming to pronounce the patient dead and finish the paperwork before starting a new day. She was a jewel.

In my second year of surgical training, I had rotations in pathology for three months and anesthesiology for three months. I got to do autopsies and look at pathologic slides in order to determine the cause of death in patients. The only good thing about the pathology rotation was that I got to do surgery even if it was on people who had recently died. We had a quota of autopsies that we tried to reach each month. Some residents told the family that a last-ditch method of treatment to save the patient's life was having them swallow a ball of pure gold. This would require an autopsy to retrieve the ball or we would have to charge the family for the gold. I found that by asking the family if they had any insurance policies on the deceased person, I usually got an autopsy. If they responded yes, I told them that I could not sign a death certificate as to the cause of death and have them receive their insurance proceeds until an autopsy was done.

In anesthesiology, I worked with anesthesiologists who kept the general surgeon's patients asleep which allowed them to do the surgery. I learned how to intubate patients, to initiate anesthesia, keep them asleep, and wake them up with no complications. Many times a patient was totally paralyzed and at the correct level of anesthesia. A belligerent surgeon, who usually either didn't know what he was doing or was having a hard time performing a certain task, would ask for more relaxation which was not possible. It gave me a new understanding about anesthesia and surgeons.

I had just finished my rotation on Pathology when I again scrubbed with Dr. Reisman. He had a patient with bilateral inguinal hernias. I repaired one side while he assisted me. After much yelling, screaming, cursing, and telling me how slow I was, I told him, "I haven't been able to do any surgery on live people for the past six months." He promptly replied, "Well, get over here on this side and do the second hernia."

Dr. Reisman was always a mentor for me and gave excellent advice on all aspects of surgery. He told me that in order to run a successful practice, you could figure that one third of your income would go to pay your staff, one third would go for income taxes to the government, and one third you got to keep. Even to this day that remains true.

Dr. Reisman was the first surgeon I saw perform bariatric surgery. He had just read about the procedure and performed an ileojejunal bypass surgery on a patient who weighed 450 pounds. This was in 1970. The surgery went well and the patient lost about 200 pounds over the next year. Only after she started drinking beer did she begin gaining weight, due to the reflux back into the bypassed small intestines. She ultimately gained all her weight back. All the diabetes and arthritis that the bypass surgery and weight loss had removed from her life came back with a vengeance.

Interestingly enough, I believe weight loss begins in your head and is the only permanent way to keep weight off. William Anderson, a licensed mental health counselor in Sarasota, Florida, has written a short book, *The Anderson Method*, that explores the causes and solutions to the problem of obesity. Using his method called "Therapeutic Psychogenics," I have lost over 135 pounds and have kept it off for over two years with no surgery. I was recently in Frisco, Texas, visiting with my son and grandson and met a bariatric surgeon who does "weight control" surgery in Dallas, Texas. We spoke about the massive number of "bypass" surgeries he does to help patients decrease their weight and thereby help with their diabetes and arthritis. He agreed that the problem is in how patients think. Surgery is not a permanent fix. Some of his patients have had five or more surgeries to try to lose weight the easy way. Most patients usually gain most of it back because their thinking and eating habits have not changed. The banding procedures or "lap band" surgery only causes a "forced starvation."

One of my favorite people whom I never met while at Erlanger Hospital was Stella the telephone operator. She was one of the people who paged doctors on an overhead paging system. She called when someone was looking for or needed the intern or resident for surgery or for the emergency room. She seemed to always be able to find us. I was walking down the hall on the seventh floor of Erlanger Hospital at midnight past an empty neurosurgical nurses station. The telephone there rang. I stopped and answered the phone and there was Stella, telling me who I needed to call or where I needed to go next.

I spent a lot of time in the X-ray department. This was before CT scans and before the Seldinger technique of puncturing an artery while introducing a catheter into the artery had come into common use. We had to do all our own arteriograms by cutting down on the brachial artery which is in the arm near the front of the elbow. We did these under the direction of the cardiovascular surgeons. It was especially important when we needed to get a splenic arteriogram or abdominal aortogram to see if the liver, spleen, or other organs in the abdomen had been ruptured. It was fascinating to be able to inject dye into the renal arteries, the splenic artery, the abdominal aorta, and even the arch of the aorta. We could occasionally snake a catheter to just above the aortic valve to get a look at the coronary arteries on the heart. The technique required opening the brachial artery in the arm to do the procedure and then repairing the artery when we finished the procedure. This was controlled practice and improved our techniques for surgery especially in emergency or vascular injury situations. Now either surgeons, intensivists, cardiologists, or interventional radiologists do the same procedures using the Seldinger technique. They can now insert stents to open up blocked arteries or bypass aneurysms.

There was a very unusual plastic surgeon who, in addition to being a very large man, had quite a large protuberant abdomen. I remember spending four long hours in the middle of the night assisting him while he sewed up multiple facial lacerations in a very pretty young female who had been in an automobile accident. As he finished the operation, he was not pleased with the results. He completely took down the repair by removing all the sutures and spent another four hours re-repairing the young girl's face. After that I was very hesitant to assist him. I walked into the operating room once to assist him doing a rhinoplasty. After I scrubbed and stood beside him in surgery at the patient's head, he said "There is not enough room at this operating table for both our bellies." After that not so subtle remark, I promptly took off my gown and gloves and left the room.

Doctors and policemen have a unique relationship. I got to know some of them very well; some I feared, and some were friends. I was driving to work early one morning just after we had moved from Cleveland to Chattanooga. I drove a used 1960 TR 3 convertible and was a little late going to work. My mind was on the schedule for surgery that day. I'm sure I was going much too fast when an approaching car turned left directly in front of me and hit my car head on. I got a large laceration to my left knee and was a little addled by the collision. The car was a total loss. I was greeted by the first cop on the scene, an officer who was well known in the emergency room. Everyone called him "Meathead."

He recognized me from the emergency room and asked me what happened. I told him that someone had pulled in front of me and I was probably speeding. He said, "Doc, the speed limit is 35 miles an hour." I responded, "Yes, Meathead. I understand that. I was probably speeding." He again stated, "Doc, the speed limit is 35 miles an hour." I finally realized what he was trying to say to me, so I stated, "I was going 35 miles an hour." That's what he put on the police report. He was trying to help me as he did most of the medical personnel he knew. I realized that I was very naive but finally figured out who the real meathead was. Secret or just lying?

The first time I scrubbed at Children's Hospital, I was still unsure of the size of gloves that I wore. One of the nurses looked at my hands and said, " You wear a size 8 glove." That's what she put on me. I wore them for the next hour during the case. When I finished, I wondered why my hands were tingling. I found that a size 8-1/2 glove was the correct size and by wearing the larger gloves, my hands no longer became numb. The same nurse incorrectly gave me a 3-0 silk suture when I had asked for a 4-0 silk suture. When I questioned her, she said I had asked for the larger suture. Rather than admitting to a mistake, she lied. Either she didn't hear me or thought I needed a larger suture. I was only a resident and she had been there for years, but I wondered why she felt it necessary to lie. Due to my naiveté, I thought surgery would be a place where people would not lie. It caused me a lot of unnecessary growing pains. I was taught in medical school and by my parents to believe that people always told the truth.

There was a tall, thin, and very pretty black scrub nurse who was married to a policeman in Chattanooga. We became friends at work because she was there a lot of times at night when we had trauma cases. She was an excellent scrub tech. She had insinuated to everyone she worked with that she and her husband had marital difficulties. She had shown up for work previously with a black eye. She told us she had been abused but had never reported this to anyone because he was a high ranking police officer and she didn't want to cause problems with his job. She had developed a deep vein thrombosis in her leg and had been treated with Warfarin, a blood thinner, for this condition. One night she came to the emergency room comatose. Her policeman husband said she had fallen down the stairs. She died within an hour. No other questions were asked. We always wondered if he had pushed her down the stairs. Deadly secrets.

An emergency room nurse who was in charge of the department became a good friend. She was an excellent teacher. She took me aside and gave me some advice when I first arrived to work in the emergency room. She said, "I know how to treat these patients. I've seen many of them many times over. If you want to get any sleep at night, let me evaluate the patients and begin treatment. I'll wake you to examine the patient and I'll have everything ready for further treatment and documentation." I found that she was almost always correct. I learned a lot of practical medicine from her. She also introduced me to Claude, who was always fighting for the "asthma chair" in the emergency room. He came in once complaining of asthma and found that someone was already seated in "his" asthma chair. He then looked at the nurse and urinated causing his pants to be soaked. He smiled and said, "My water broke." That didn't help him get in "his" asthma chair.

Nothing has changed with patients waiting to be seen in the emergency room. By law you cannot refuse to see patients because they have no insurance. Some of them will get tired of waiting to be seen, leave, go home, and call 911 so they can return to the ER and be seen first even if they have nonemergencies. In a doctor's office or clinic, arrangements would have to be made for payment for service. The ER is "free." It doesn't matter what the charge is if the patient won't pay. In my training, we spent a lot of time talking to and examining the patients. It seems that today the emergency room doctors order tests and X-rays and occasionally examine patients. I actually had a patient here in Clewiston who was in an automobile accident and had a questionable concussion. The ER doctor ordered a CT of her head, a CT of her neck, a CT of her chest, a CT of her abdomen and pelvis. To give you some relative comparisons, one CT exam is the equivalent amount of radiation you get from one hundred chest X-rays. This patient received the equivalent radiation of four hundred chest X-rays with the CT scans she received. When I admitted her for observation overnight for her concussion, she asked me, "Dr. Carroll, why didn't anyone touch me in the emergency room?" I think most of the problems now in our emergency rooms stem from fear of litigation. Sometimes I think the multiple tests and X-rays are used to CYA.

Growing up, I never attended a movie until I was twelve years old. One of the rules I had been taught in church was that movies were sinful and not to be attended. The movie was in Cinerama with a larger screen and Surround Sound and included a roller coaster ride. I thought the ceiling in the movie theater would collapse and kill me. I felt very guilty even though I thoroughly enjoyed the movie.

I rarely went to any movies after that first experience. A group from the emergency room, including the chief nurse, asked me to go with them to a local "art theater" where the movie *Deep Throat* was playing. Obviously I was a very naïve young physician and was filled with shame and trepidation the entire time we were there. About halfway through the movie, there was a police raid. The chief nurse's husband, a police officer, came in through a back door and gathered all of the emergency room people including me, his wife, and several others. We slipped unnoticed out the same back door. The rest of the audience was directed out the front door to waiting newspaper photographers and reporters. Pictures and names of the people attending the movie were on the front page of the next morning's newspaper. I narrowly missed a most embarrassing experience. Can you imagine an incident like that happening now? Another secret that was never mentioned until now.

At Christmas time during my last year at Erlanger Hospital, all the usual hospital parties were being scheduled. Everyone thought that being my size, I would be an excellent Santa Claus and one of the new interns would be Santa's elf. We would appear at the Christmas party for the residents and interns and the attending surgical staff doctors . We would pass out gifts after the dinner. The night of the party, my elf became quite inebriated. After having at least six gin and tonics, he got rather loud and boisterous. On several occasions he was offensive to our attending doctors. His father was an older general practitioner in town who also did surgery and I guess he assumed that he could get away with anything. One of the doctors that my elf was giving an extremely difficult time was the resident in general surgery in Memphis who got in trouble with Dr. Wilson at one of our surgical "prayer meetings" in medical school. After finishing his residency in Memphis, he had moved to Chattanooga to begin his surgical practice. He thought very well of himself and was chief of surgery at Erlanger Hospital. My helper elf had planned to play Fats Domino's song "I'm Gonna Be a Wheel Someday, I'm Going To Be Somebody" and dedicate it to the surgeon. It almost caused a fight between us but I prevented him from doing it. I wasn't going to lose my job for that. Since I had four children at the time, Santa gave number one a lifetime prescription for birth control pills.

The rest of the story came about the next morning when it was my responsibility to assign the interns to the surgical cases they were to scrub on. Santa's helper was assigned to a neurosurgical case. After he vomited in the scrub sink in front of the neurosurgeon, he realized he was in trouble.

However, he went ahead and assisted on the case for several hours until close to lunchtime. He was still not feeling well and I received a call that he needed to be replaced for lunch. I assigned another resident to replace him. When my elf was relieved at lunch, he immediately went to his quarters, got in bed, and went soundly to sleep. Eight hours later when the neurosurgical case finally finished, the resident whom I had assigned to complete the case with the neurosurgeon was quite unhappy and was looking for my elf to "discuss" the situation with him. Again, I had to cover myself and my elf just to keep the peace.

I had a visiting resident from England ask to borrow my new

two-door blue straight shift Chevy. I felt really bad that he had no means of transportation and lent him my car which he wrecked approximately four hours later. My loss.

We had an epidemic of prisoners begin coming to the ER from jail. Each had a fever and a markedly elevated white count indicating sepsis or an infection somewhere. A syringe that had been brought in by a visitor or stolen from the infirmary would be filled with "spit." Then the prisoner would inject their own saliva or even another inmate's saliva in their lower leg, causing a large abscess. After using a local anesthetic agent, the surgery resident would open the abscess by using a scalpel and drain the pus. Usually they were admitted to the surgical ward on the third floor of the hospital for IV antibiotics. Since we had no air conditioning, the prisoners excelled at slipping out an open window, dropping down to the second floor over the emergency room, then down to the ground where they could escape from both the hospital and jail. You could not do it today, but the chief resident stopped the influx of prisoners by opening an abscess without local anesthesia. The patient screamed due to the pain. Then the resident told him, "Go back and tell everyone how bad it hurts!" That stopped the problem.

The hospital CEO would not buy an air-conditioning unit for indigent patients. We devised a plan that worked. We called the newspaper and had a reporter and photographer come to the hospital to his office where we presented the CEO $200 in pennies in a wheelbarrow. The residents and interns had bought the first air-conditioning unit for the surgical ward.

I needed to work extra as often as I could. I enjoyed working in the emergency room and especially enjoyed the trauma. I remember my father coming to visit me while I was working one afternoon. He didn't want to participate but only wanted to stand in the corner of the room and watch while I sutured a laceration. He seemed to enjoy watching what maybe he could have been doing if he hadn't been called to the ministry. I think he was actually proud of me.

I was working late one night when a young man was brought in by an ambulance. He had been shot with a .25 caliber "Saturday night special" revolver. We worked with him but to no avail. I finally pronounced him dead. Everybody was upset about the murder. We learned that the young man had been shot in the chest while standing in the street. It was difficult to believe the story we learned over the course of the next thirty minutes. As the group of people he worked with came in the emergency room, the complete story came out. This young man was the director of a group that was raising money for a local halfway house in the inner-city. He had worked it out with one of his street people to shoot him with his own small .25 caliber handgun. The plan was that he would be injured and could use the disability insurance money for building the inner-city halfway house. The person picked to be involved with this scam had actually missed the young man's arm or leg and shot him in the chest, causing his accidental death.

A sixteen-year-old girl who had been killed in an automobile accident one block from her home was brought in. That day had been her sixteenth birthday. In order to set up a surprise birthday party for her daughter, the mother had asked her daughter's boyfriend to drive the "birthday girl" around the block. There was a bad accident. The boyfriend didn't have a scratch but the sixteen-year-old girl was dead. We spent the next hour trying to get the mother to understand that her daughter had been killed. She could not handle the truth and kept repeating that she needed to get back home for a surprise birthday party for her daughter.

A set of fraternal twins came in the ER at Children's Hospital. They were six years old and just started to school. The mother and father had gone through a very bitter divorce and the mother had gotten custody of the children. That morning the kids had gone outside to wait for the school bus. As the school bus arrived, they ran together across the street toward the bus. Both were hit by an oncoming car that had not slowed down and stopped for the bus. I took the son to surgery but his liver and spleen were ruptured. He died during surgery. The six-year-old sister had a successful operation. When I gave the news to the waiting mother and father along with their new separate families, a fight broke out in the waiting room. Hospital security had to be called in to separate the mother and father.

A new resident came on staff when I was chief surgical resident, an older physician from the state of Mississippi. He had been in practice for fifteen years and wanted to come back for two years of surgical training. If he did this, he could return to the rural area where he lived and do surgery in addition to his family practice. One morning he came into the emergency room where I was seeing a patient. He had been up all night and I noticed he was carrying a chest X-ray. Putting the X-ray on the viewing box, I said, "Well, your patient has a pneumothorax on the right side and you have a chest tube on the left side. You have taken care of the problem on the left and you have one more to correct on the right. Put in another chest tube on the right." His response was, "I thought I was doing that with the first chest tube, but I put it in the wrong side. I'll go back and take it out." I quickly responded, "No. No. That's not the correct thing to do. You'll have to leave the first one in and go back and put a chest tube in the side you thought you were doing the first time." When the case came to surgical mortality and morbidity conference that week, he was expecting multiple questions concerning his decision-making by our attending staff. However he defused the entire situation and started his presentation by saying, "I made a mistake. I put a chest tube in the wrong side of my patient initially." This truth neutralized most of the venom from the responses of the rest of the doctors and made his first mortality and morbidity conference a memorable one for all of us. The truth had set him free.

Usually before, but occasionally during surgery, I could tell if a physician I was going to assist had been imbibing alcoholic beverages. It was obvious by the smell of his breath and by his slowed actions. I noticed on one occasion a cardiovascular physician and a pump technician who appeared to be inebriated while carrying out a coronary artery bypass graft. The technician sometimes would be so drunk that he would have blackout spells for three to four days at a time and never even remember where he had been or what he had been doing. Even during those times,

I never saw him not be able to handle the bypass machine correctly and never saw a patient lost by that physician or the technician because of their inebriation.

We did have a general surgeon who came in on a Saturday morning to perform surgery. Before his case got started he asked, "Dr. Carroll, have you ever done an above-the-knee amputation?" I responded that I had. He then explained, "Well, it has been quite a hot day and I've been out in the garden and had a few more beers than I needed to. If you can do this, I would like to stand and watch." I operated on his patient. He never attempted to help or do the surgery himself because, in his opinion, he was not capable of performing the operation correctly and didn't want to harm his patient.

These two cases represented extremes. It also taught me to be very open and honest in admitting problems or possible complications in surgery that could arise.

A surgeon had attended a week-long surgical meeting out of state with his wife. On coming home he made a trip to the local pornographic bookstore on a Sunday afternoon. He was found dead in a movie viewing room. He evidently was a friend of the store owner and when the owner found his body, instead of calling the police, he called the surgeon's partners. They came and removed the body and carried it to the surgeon's office. I don't think the police were ever involved but I'm quite sure this should have been reported and could have caused possible problems because the body was moved after death. But at least the partners kept the physician's reputation somewhat intact by doing this. Another instance of a secret kept.

One of the thoracic surgeons had a large house on Lake Chickamauga. He and his wife noticed a boat floating past his property one bright sunny afternoon. The boat had possibly come loose from a neighbor's dock. They got in their boat and while approaching the other boat, the physician saw what appeared to be a man lying in the bottom of the boat. On closer examination, he noticed a man lying on top of a woman. Trying to be funny, he yelled, "Are you catching anything?" The man looked up and replied, "I certainly hope not."

One of the interns on my surgical service had had his leg amputated in his teen years because of an osteogenic sarcoma, which is a bad-acting malignant tumor. He had an above-the-knee prosthesis that he wore at times but didn't like. Most of the time he was able to get around quite well just with crutches. He told me that he had a patient in the clinic who had lymphoma and had pleural effusions on both sides of his chest. We talked about the situation. I explained that this was a patient we had followed for a long time and these were chronic recurrent pleural effusions secondary to his lymphoma. In addition he had had multiple treatments with chemotherapy and a very poor prognosis. I instructed the intern to go to the emergency room and remove the fluid from one side of the patient's chest. I explained one of the possible complications of the procedure was collapsing a lung. If there were any such problem, only one side would be affected. When he came back an hour later, he was very excited to tell me that he had done such a good job on one side that he went ahead and drew fluid out of other side of the chest also. Very calmly I told him that one or both lungs could possibly collapse, as I had previously told him. "No, that could never happen," he said. One and a half hours later the patient came back to the emergency room DOA with both lungs collapsed. What a tough lesson for an intern to learn. You must follow specific orders.

As a senior resident, my responsibilities and experiences increased. I was able to perform many surgeries especially those received in traumatic situations. A young man came to the emergency room after having a motorcycle accident. I got a stat call to go to the trauma side of the emergency room. A fourteen-year-old male had a very bad leg injury. However, we were taught to look at the person as a whole and not be distracted by obvious injuries. On examining his very tight abdomen, it was elementary that he had internal hemorrhaging probably from a ruptured spleen. This was in the early 1970s before CT scans, arteriograms, and attempts to salvage the spleen were used routinely. After a thorough exam, I took the patient to surgery. There was no anesthesiology resident available. After talking quickly to one of the attending anesthesiologists, he was willing to help us due to the emergency. The young man had no identification and we assumed no insurance but needed immediate surgery. On opening his abdomen, the young man's spleen was completely shattered and a splenectomy was carried out. He required several units of blood during surgery. As I was finishing the case and making plans to call orthopedics for his damaged leg, the attending surgeon who was the chief of surgery at that time scrubbed and walked into the operating room. (I became his partner in private practice several years later.) He watched me very intently and said, "Do you need some help?" I responded, "Of course, his spleen was ruptured and I just got it out." Together we finished the case. During the rest of the surgery he told me that this young man was the son of one of the most prominent attorneys in town and that maybe I had acted rashly by taking the patient to surgery without asking for assistance of one of the attending surgeons. I countered that the young man had no identification, that nothing indicated his "insurance status." I had thought he was an indigent patient but had realized that he needed immediate surgery due to his life-threatening situation. It was quite a surprise several months later when the patient and his father came back to the hospital and paged me. Both the attorney and his fourteen-year-old son, who was still on crutches, shook my hand and thanked me for being present for the initial operation and helping save the son's life.

One of the attending radiologists was well noted for being "wishy-washy" on his diagnoses. I presented a case from the emergency room to him as he had performed the X-rays on the patient. He told me personally that the spleen was ruptured and that I needed to take the patient to surgery. Sometimes it can be very difficult to tell on physical exam if there really is an internal problem. When I took the patient to surgery, there was not a ruptured spleen and in fact there was nothing abnormal in the abdomen. I went back down to X-ray and explained this to the radiologist. He stated, "I know, I just looked at the CT again and I'm going to put in my report that everything was normal." I was adamant about the fact that he must dictate the report as he had told me in person. He finally relented but I often thought if I had not gone back and talked to him, I would've been totally responsible for a negative exploration of the patient. I lost a lot of respect for him. Hindsight is 20-20.

In the teaching aspect of my duties as a chief resident, I had one of the first-year surgery residents get a history from, perform a physical on, and diagnose, a patient. He told me that he believed the patient had appendicitis. I asked one of the third-year surgery residents to go ahead and start the surgery. At the operation, they could not find the appendix. I came in and explored the entire right lower quadrant of the abdomen including the retroperitoneal area. No appendix was found. As we were closing the incision, I asked about the scar in the right lower part of the abdomen. The resident stated that the patient told him that he had cut his stomach while going through a barbed wire fence. When he awoke, it was obvious that the patient had been lying. He finally admitted he just wanted the pain medication. Again we were taught to believe the patient, but learned that sometimes they lie.

I once stayed up for fifty four hours straight while working in the clinic, ER, and OR. It actually was an exhausting experience. I could not readily go to sleep when I had a chance to lie down. Eventually I was able to sleep from early afternoon until 7:00 the next morning. Surgical training required long hours especially for continuity of care. It was important to follow a patient from the initial exam through the entire course of their stay in the hospital. A famous case in New York City later made surgical training programs change their entire setup. Rules were established. No one could work over twenty four hours continuously. When the twenty four hours ended, you must leave and go home. I would have fought someone if he had tried to take away any surgery that I worked up all night and was taking to surgery the next morning. In my opinion, these rules cause a loss in the continuity of care and in the basic training of general surgeons. Tendencies now are to go back to the original way surgeons were trained. Studies have shown that there is no difference in the surgery done after someone has been awake for twenty four hours and someone who operated freshly in the morning. There may be some decrease in reaction time, but no measurable increase in complications for any type of surgery.

One of the most rewarding cases I ever did was a case that my Aunt Odine sent me- a five-year-old little boy from Haiti who had a large right inguinal hernia. He had no insurance and by working with Erlanger Hospital, I was able to repair his hernia without charge. Fifteen years later he came back to thank me. I considered that better payment than the insurance company could have provided.

Sometimes we were asked to assist in getting the patient from the emergency room to the OB floor when they were in the process of having a baby. One of the things that the expectant delivering mother was told included, "Breathe through your mouth, Mother, don't push." One night we were helping the OB/GYN resident take his patient to the elevators to go up to the obstetrical suite. As the door was closing I said, "Push, Mother, push," just trying to be funny. To my surprise I learned that the baby had been born on the elevator.

I was called to the emergency room stat one morning and found one of my best friends there. He was a surgical tech whom I had worked with many times. He was a motorcycle fanatic. He rode to the hospital every day and passed by the road leading to my house. He had been run off the road by a car and had landed in someone's front yard. I had passed a motorcycle wreck that morning going to work. My friend was brought in shortly after I got to the hospital. He was in shock from internal bleeding. I placed a chest tube because of a hemopneumothorax and immediately got copious amounts of blood. I'll never forget his last words, "Leonard, I'm hurting really bad." He passed away before we could do anything further or take him to surgery to stop the bleeding. He did not respond to our resuscitation.

We were making rounds on the indigent ward one morning with all the residents and interns present. One of the questions we asked all the patients who had abdominal surgery to see if their bowels had resumed working was, "Have you passed any gas through your rectum?" The first person to be seen on rounds that morning was a patient who had surgery two days prior and was asked, "Have you passed any gas?" The response I got was, "Not me, Doc. It must have been that guy in the next bed."

Sometimes it was difficult to get the patients to follow the orders given to the nurses. The indigent ward had thirty beds around the walls of the room. There was a table between each bed with water, food, or equipment. If the patient was NPO (nothing by mouth) for whatever reason, his table was empty. But it was very easy for him to reach the table on the other side of his bed and drink his neighbor's water.

For the 11:00 PM to 7:00 AM shift, two surgical suites were kept open for emergency surgery. There were twenty-two operating rooms in the entire surgical suite. Most of the rooms were unused at night especially the back rooms 20, 21, and 22. On several occasions, residents were known to use local anesthesia and do vasectomies on other residents or interns. I was one of those in late 1971. The older resident from Mississippi was another even though he complained that his semiannual erection had become an annual semierection. These again were secrets that were never exposed. I don't think the Mississippi resident ever told his family that he had had a vasectomy. The OR supervisor was Mrs. Romans. She made accusations regarding our use or misuse of these rooms. Never once did we admit to anything but I think we never fully convinced her that we weren't doing outpatient surgery on other residents and interns in those rooms.

On one occasion, a fellow chief resident assisted me on an unusual case. A technician in the X-ray department had asked if we could perform a hysterectomy on her cat. I had never done any veterinary work, but we agreed that his responsibility was to use open-drop ether on the cat while I did the surgery. He found it necessary to put on lead-lined gloves from the X-ray department in order to hold the cat until the ether took effect. Getting and keeping the cat asleep was difficult; it was a simple process to make a lower midline incision and do the hysterectomy.

The cat survived and no one was ever the wiser as to what we carried out in the X-ray department late that night.

I was in the operating room on one occasion with the chief of staff at Erlanger and my future partner in private practice. We were scrubbed on a case when the "floating nurse" rushed into the room and said, "Dr. B, one of the residents has started an IV on a baby in the intensive care unit and the baby's leg has turned black." Dr. B immediately turned to me and said, "I'll finish here. Get over there and see what's happening." I knew better than to question him and immediately broke scrub and went to the intensive care unit. I found a foreign resident there who had done a surgical "cut down," or surgically exposed a vein, so a catheter could be placed in the vein and IV fluids be given. He had used the groin rather than at the ankle where we usually did "cut downs." The resident didn't understand the anatomy of the area. He had placed a suture around the femoral vein in the baby's leg, causing the leg to be a dark blue. It was necessary for me to recognize what he had done, see where the suture had been placed around the large vein, and then to take the suture off the vein. Over the next few minutes baby's leg pinked back up. Coincidence or miracle?

We had to fill many of the open resident positions with foreign medical graduates. It seemed that their outlook on life in general was totally different from ours. I always thought and still believe that surgical decisions should be made in conjunction with the patient and his wishes. Just because he had a hernia or gallbladder full of stones didn't mean that surgery had to be done immediately. We should at least ask the patient what he wanted done, explaining the surgery and possible complications, and together arrive at a decision about operating. Many times it seemed that a foreign medical graduate's attitude was "If I'm in training and you have a hernia or gallbladder with stones or other operable condition, you must train me so I'll operate no matter what you think." This is a vulnerable time for patients. I recently had a surgical consult here in Florida. The patient was ninety years old and had both a very large hernia and gallbladder disease with stones. Neither problem bothered him. He asked me, "Doc, do I have to have these problems operated on? They don't bother me." He would have let me operate and Medicare would have paid me. I told him. "I'll do whatever you want." He was thrilled not to have surgery. I followed him for the next two years and he died peacefully at home with no further problems from either his hernia or gallbladder.

Often when surgery was slow and we wanted to break the monotony, we would take the plastic casing for a Fogarty balloon catheter, which was approximately three feet long, and was discarded after the catheter had been used on a previous case. There was a larger area on one end where the catheter was placed in. It was obvious to me that this appeared to be and would become a perfect blowgun. When we carefully cut off the small end of the long tube and placed in the homemade dart made from a six-inch Q tip and 18-gauge needle, it became usable. You could then sneak up to the roof of the hospital where there were pigeons. After several practice shots, you could become pretty good at hitting pigeons with a homemade dart gun although I don't think we ever killed one. When we had free time, we could use the beautiful heavy antique billiard table along with the coffee pot, ping-pong table, TV set, and lounge chairs in the residents' lounge.

We always kidded the older resident who came from Mississippi about taking so much time in the bathroom at the residents' quarters. At one point we threw a lighted Cherry bomb in the all-ceramic bathroom while he was there. The explosion reverberated for what seemed like forever. He acted as if nothing had happened, but for a moment we thought we had injured him. Stupid but I guess "All's well that ends well."

My first subclavian catheter insertion was in 1968. Dr. Stanley Dudrick had published a paper that described how he had raised a group of basset puppies using total parenteral nutrition and not feeding them at all by mouth. In order to do this, you must access a large central (close to the heart) vein (usually the subclavian vein underneath the collar bone) and place a large catheter into the vein. You can give nutrients such as protein (amino acids) and sugar (dextrose) intravenously to allow someone to heal wounds while they have no oral intake. It was used extensively in soldiers injured in the Viet Nam war. As residents we read the initial article and went to the morgue in the hospital to learn how to insert the catheters on patients recently passed away. I still use the same method now that I learned in 1968.

In 1968, I was asked to start a methadone clinic in Chattanooga. There was an epidemic of heroin usage and one of the newer methods of treating heroin addiction was described by Drs. Dole and Nyswander. They replaced the heroin addiction by giving methadone, an opiate, which had no associated euphoria and blocked the euphoria of heroin. Several of the narcotic addicts did not believe this and actually overdosed by injecting massive amounts of heroin trying to obtain the usual euphoria associated with the heroin use. Two addicts actually died from their overdose. Methadone allowed a person to work and not become dependent on illegal drugs and society. I met a young Jewish social worker who was exactly the same age as I. We had been born approximately two hours apart in different parts of the country. Coincidence? We traveled to New Orleans to visit a methadone clinic started by the original doctors who wrote the paper. We came back and instituted the same thing in Chattanooga in 1968. It was necessary to get a special narcotic license to use methadone in this manner. The only available form to use at that time was a thick cherry-flavored syrup that was difficult for most of the heroin addicts to keep on their stomach without medication to prevent nausea.

We worked to help as many patients as possible to break their habit. Methadone did and still does work well. In my opinion, it replaces one addiction with another manageable one. I believe that faith-based programs have the least incidence of recidivism. Jesus Christ can fill the "God-sized hole" in every addicted person's life.

We had integrated a basketball team along with the drug rehabilitation program to relieve some of the frequently associated aggression. I remember on one occasion playing a game in a small gymnasium in the inner city. The game was brutal and I had to take one of the players to the ER after the game for repair of a laceration to his eyebrow. One of the older addicts, "Jughead," said, "Don't worry, Doc, I have my gun with me if things get bad." I spoke with many organizations in town to help with the awareness of the heroin problem.

We even got together what I called Dr. Carroll's traveling show which included a young black man 6 feet 7 inches tall and one hundred forty pounds nicknamed "Stick," a pretty eighteen-year-old white girl with blond hair, and an older heavyset black woman who could steal anything from any place of business in town. My team and I would travel to different locations to speak and answer questions about opiate addiction in order to educate people on the dangers of drug usage. LSD was widely used at this time also. Some of the most vivid and colorful descriptions of dreams or visions I've ever heard were associated with LSD trips. Some people could see the singing group come out of the record album, stand in front of them, and see the words as letters of the alphabet as they came out of their mouths. Most of the trips were beautiful, but ten to fifteen percent of the dreams involved helicopters with steel jaws chasing the drug user. Most did not enjoy such Technicolor dreams. One of the ways the drug suppliers paid workers who prepared LSD for street sale by placing a drop of LSD on a small clay tablet was by letting them lick their fingers at the end of a shift.

We would take the traveling show out to Eastgate Mall in Chattanooga and notify the police about what we were going to do. The team would illustrate how addicts could "boost" or steal anything they were asked to from any of the stores in the mall. One Saturday afternoon we went to the mall for such a demonstration and had them bring out many thousands of dollars in stolen goods and clothing and place them in a pile in front of the policemen. We tried to help the police show consumers and average citizens the extent of the problem with drug usage and it's associated costs.

In my opinion marijuana was always considered the gateway drug to opiates, hallucinogenics, benzos, or amphetamines, because the person who sold marijuana had all the other drugs or could make them available. There was also cocaine usage. In my training, I spent Saturday mornings assisting the attending plastic surgeons set broken noses. Cocaine is a local anesthetic and came as crystals. When mixed with saline and epinephrine, it was used while repairing fractures of the nose. By using the local anesthesia, the patients did not have to be put to sleep. The epinephrine kept the person's nose from bleeding badly. The cocaine made them so high they didn't mind someone setting their broken nose. I watched an elderly black orderly who cleaned the rooms between the cases take the residual cocaine crystals or liquid to sale it and supplement his salary. He was eventually caught and fired. In fifty years I have only seen two people die from a ruptured heart; both were associated with cocaine usage which caused the heart to contract forcefully against closed heart valves.

At that time, most of the drugs were used and sold on 9th Street, renamed later Martin Luther King Junior Boulevard. I spent several nights there working with my patients and even shooting pool in a local bar. It's amazing how a large white man in a white shirt will stand out under an ultraviolet light in a nightclub. The addicts appreciated my being there and trying to understand the scope of the drug problem in their lives.

Two of the very colorful characters I met while running the methadone clinic were "June" and "Bunny." Both were young black men. One was rather tall and fair skinned while the other was short and dark. They would use a "mish" which they told me was a roll of paper surrounded by dollar bills in all denominations giving the appearance of wealth. This would attract men and enticed them to use their services. They would tape their scrotal contents toward their belly and would pretend to be women. They would get a man drunk and "roll him" which meant they would steal all his money. It was interesting to have them come to the clinic where everyone in the methadone program had to "pee in a cup". This was the original drug screening test that everyone took and each person had to be observed while urinating.

Many times in order to get a "clean urine," an addict would get a friend who was not a drug addict to urinate and then place the urine in their own bladder with a Foley catheter or bring in a plastic bag with urine taped to their abdomen to keep the urine warm. If no one observed them urinating, they could get a negative drug screen. June and Bunny would come dressed in colorful dresses and I would have to go into the restroom with them and observe their urinating in a cup. They always thought this was hilarious. Bunny was unfortunate enough to get granuloma venereum which is a sexually transmitted disease. It affected his rectum so badly that he had to have a colostomy. His spirit never weakened and he always spoke of his colostomy as "a little business on the side." Humor, coping, or sick business?

I watched a twenty-five-year-old male who could not do fractions and knew very little math at at all. He only completed the third grade and learned how to add and multiply fractions by measuring out partial teaspoons of heroin. He knew that one fourth and one fourth equaled one half. I was in the hospital when a nurse mistakenly overdosed and inadvertently killed a patient. She didn't know her fractions. She thought one half grain of morphine added to one half grain morphine gave her the correct dose of one fourth grain of morphine. When she gave the incorrect dose intravenously to a patient, he stopped breathing. This young heroin addict would take his love for codeine to unbelievable levels. He would forge prescriptions of codeine cough syrup or liquid codeine pain medication and get the prescription filled at a local drugstore. He would go into the pharmacy with an identical brown bottle filled with 4 ounces of dark Karo syrup in his pocket. When he got his codeine prescription, he would switch bottles and placed the bottle of dark Karo syrup in the white pharmacy bag, turn around, trip and fall. Dropping the bottle inside the bag on the floor caused the bottle to break and fill the bag with liquid. The pharmacist would notice that he had ruined his medication and would refill the codeine for him. This very street-smart young man then had two bottles of liquid codeine cough syrup instead of one.

I watched a black man and white woman go into a jewelry store pretending to look at engagement rings. The young lady would actually cut a round opening in an orange to suck the juice out. She would take the orange with her when they entered the store. While the couple was looking at engagement rings, the young man would reach over the counter and distract the salesperson. While he did this, the young lady would place a diamond engagement ring inside the orange. When the salesperson looked up, she would walk to the front door and throw out the orange with the diamond ring inside to a waiting accomplice outside. These young people were not stupid but very ingenious. They were addicts.

These and many other such experiences led me to become board certified in addiction medicine by the American Board of Addiction Medicine as well as being board certified by the American College of Surgery.

I had my first exposure to malpractice in the early 1960s. Two well-known surgeons from Chattanooga were sued. A colorectal surgeon had a patient who needed to have his hemorrhoids removed and a general surgeon had a patient who needed a testicle removed for malignancy. The two patients were inadvertently switched outside surgery and the patient who needed the malignant testicle removed got a hemorrhoid-ectomy and the patient who needed a hemorrhoidectomy got his testicle removed. Operating on the accidently switched patients caused a large malpractice suit. It made the cover of *Time* magazine. Both physicians were sued but readily admitted that bad publicity was better than no publicity at all. After this incident, both of their practices took off like a rocket. The general surgeon had a partner who thought this ultimate fame was good for both of them but let notoriety go to his head. We used to say among ourselves about the partner, "there but for the grace of God goes God." On the malpractice side, I observed a neurosurgeon who operated and drilled burr holes on the wrong side of the skull to relieve a subdural hematoma and an orthopedist who operated on the wrong knee. Secrets were present and still are in the practice of general surgery. Now we are told to be forthcoming to a patient's family and tell the truth. Imagine that!

In 1970 *Jesus Christ Superstar* by Andrew Lloyd Weber and Tim Rice became a national phenomenon. I thoroughly enjoyed the fact that the musical very closely followed biblical dialogue and story. By the time it came to Chattanooga as a rock opera production, I went by myself to Memorial Auditorium in Chattanooga. I knew all the lyrics and enjoyed singing along with the entire production. When I left the auditorium there was a group from a local church standing on the steps of the Auditorium and singing hymns in protest to the secularization of Jesus Christ. I stood and sang with the choir all the verses of "Amazing Grace." I had no problems with the rock opera because of my solid foundations and belief in Jesus Christ. I always figured this was an opportunity to spread Jesus' fame further.

One of the major transitions in my life happened when my father passed away on 29 January 1972 in the last year of my surgical training. I received an ominous call on a Wednesday evening. My father had just returned from Greenville, South Carolina. He had gone to the same church where he had preached his first sermon at eighteen years of age. He also preached the last sermon of his life there at age fifty-one. He had visited the church as the general overseer of the Church of God. He came home with my mother to Cleveland, Tennessee. They went to bed early because Dad said he was tired. When he complained of chest pain and being unable to breathe, my mother called 911 and an ambulance was sent. Dad was transported to Cleveland Memorial Hospital. I got my call from the hospital. I was told that my father was not doing well. I raced the 23 miles to the hospital and had a state trooper following me. On pulling into the parking lot at the hospital, I jumped out of my car and ran with the trooper chasing me. When he realized the situation, he stopped his pursuit. I went into the emergency room where a resident in anesthesiology at Erlanger had been "moonlighting" in the ER. He had actually waited for me to get there to pronounce my own father! I had to do this and then walk out and tell my mother that Dad was dead. She was surrounded by many friends. I know it was difficult for her and is still a very vivid memory in my life today. I then had to organize his funeral. The cost involved with the funeral—from the suggestion that the concrete vault needed to be painted gold and a bronze plaque with Dad's name engraved on it to the extra cost of "opening a grave" on a weekend—was unbelievable! I asked the funeral director, "Who will ever go down there to look at the vault or plaque?" The cheapest appropriate coffin I could buy, a spray of yellow roses (Dad's favorite flowers), and a trip to Greenville, South Carolina, for his burial there, caused me a lot of anger and mixed emotions. I could have bought Mother a new car for what we spent.

The transition between the last two years of my residency or surgical training and the first year of my two years in the Army were the most difficult times of my life. This portion of my life is filled with secrets that were never been openly discussed with anyone. I think it has something to do with the shame and guilt associated with my foolish, misguided, rebellious decisions. I did not listen to advice. I got married in the interim between when I failed out of medical school and started again in March 1964. I was married to number one in December 1963. We had four children, in the next six years, along with many other problems. Two were born while I was in medical school, a daughter in April 1965 and a son in May 1967, just before I graduated in June. Things were actually so confusing during that time that only when I started researching did I find there was a divorce filed by number one in late 1968 or early 1969 and then rescinded several months after it was filed. I had a second son born in May 1969 and things at home rapidly disintegrated. A divorce was finalized in late 1969. For several months after the divorce I was left alone. Things had gotten so bad that my feelings of abandonment reemerged. I remarried number one in July 1970 in Chattanooga. The ceremony was performed by a minister friend of my father's. My third son was born in June 1971. In less than seven months, my father had passed away and I had gone through the second divorce from number one.

My father had performed my first marriage with number one in Lenoir City, Tennessee. He had drawn a diagram on the front blank page of his Bible showing the union of me and number one with our first three offspring. I noticed this when my mother gave me my father's Bible after his death in 1972. This diagram showed a double dividing line between number one and me when we obtained the first divorce. I also noticed that Dad had filled in our remarriage in 1970 and the birth of my fourth child in June 1971 in his Bible.

I felt extremely depressed and even found it difficult to attempt to maintain any relationship after realizing how my father had actually perceived the divorce and remarriage. These were tumultuous times and the fact that I was going in the Army and didn't know exactly where I would be sent added to the stress. As I stated before, I asked the US Army in early 1972 to send me anywhere in the world, from Vietnam, Korea, Japan, to Germany; preferably anywhere oversees. The Army, in all their wisdom, sent me from Chattanooga, Tennessee, to Huntsville, Alabama, approximately one hundred ten miles away.

CHAPTER 11

My father passed away in January 1972. Between then and the conclusion of the second divorce from number one in June 1972, I continued a friendship with number two. She had been married to a physician who had attended medical school in Korea because he could not obtain admission to a US medical school. After coming back from Korea, he started his training at Erlanger Hospital. I was a third year surgery resident when he came as an intern. We talked a lot and we became friends. He had shared with me the difficulties of getting in medical school in the United States and his reasoning for going to medical school in Korea. Number two worked as a graphic illustrator for the Army while they were in Korea. She had a child just before moving back to the States that was either miscarried, aborted, or given up for adoption. I never got the full story. Number two knew at that time that her husband had Hodgkin's disease. He had canceled his one life insurance policy for $200,000 before he found out about his illness. When he passed away, number two was left penniless and dependent on her own devices. She got a job at a Chattanooga newspaper. Number two had many problems of her own. She was manic-depressive—now called bipolar. She was described as "bubbly" when she was high or manic. I never saw her in the depths of depression except when she refused to take her medication and then she would usually isolate. She called me one Sunday afternoon and asked me to come over to her house. There were two resident friends who were in the room when I got the call and strongly advised me not to visit her. They felt she was attempting to attract me and knew she wanted to marry another doctor. I thought I could help. I could not be dissuaded. Boy, was I wrong. Bad mistake.

Coincidence or miracle? But if I had not taken that direction, I probably would not be where I am today. Romans 8:26 says "Everything works together for good to him who loves the Lord."

Number two had what she described as several episodes of molestation and sexual abuse as a teenager by her father. She had written a lengthy treatise to document this. I tried to get a copy to keep in a safe place but she refused and kept it at home. As an adult she he had an almost nonexistent relationship with her father. Studies show that a young girl is most likely to get pregnant between 3:00 PM and 5:00 PM in the afternoon, in her own home while both parents are working and not there, and the first time she has intercourse. To attest to all these facts, number two became pregnant as a teenager by a young man who was planning to and eventually did become a doctor, after school at her house while her parents were working, and she said it was the first time she had had intercourse. Her boyfriend never acknowledged being the father of the child. She was forced by her father to leave home and go to a Salvation Army Hospital in Kentucky and to remain there alone until the baby was born. Her mother and father never visited. Several weeks later she and the baby appeared before a judge and the little boy was adopted. She was then allowed to come home.

To my knowledge she never once attempted to find out about the child or allow him to find her. I should have seen the warning signs but did not.

As our relationship intensified, I received a letter from the United States Army asking me to show up in Huntsville, Alabama, at Redstone Arsenal on 1 July, 1972. Not knowing what else to do, not wanting to be alone, and wanting to stay in contact with my four children, I took number two with me to Redstone Arsenal. We were not married but told the Army we were. This was an unbelievable secret foisted on the Army. It was not until 18 August 1972 that I married number two. She had picked 18 August for us to get married because it was number one's birthday. Coincidence? Looking back, I think it was sick and done on purpose.

I was given visitation rights with my children after the second divorce from number one. I drove back and forth from Huntsville to Chattanooga every other week even during the times of President Ford's gas rationing when gas sold for $3.33 a gallon. My Chevrolet station wagon would get me from Huntsville to Chattanooga to pick up my four children and bring them back to Redstone Arsenal. I could refill with gas when I got back on the Army base. You can imagine things were rather rocky during this period of time.

There was much verbal abuse from both myself and number two. We had multiple counseling sessions by chaplains in the Army but nothing appeared to work. We were divorced in February 1973 only six months after marrying. I found that my children were very tolerant and would go along with almost any situation if they realized they were loved. I loved my kids.

I had begun a coin collection many years before with my father and maintained it after his death. I carried it with me to Huntsville. On obtaining a divorce from number two, she did everything possible to manipulate me. She secretly hid my coin collection, stamp collection, and other things that were more valuable to me sentimentally than monetarily. Following the pattern of number one, I was remarried to number two in March 1973 less than one month after the divorce. I should have been able to fend for myself but maintained a very unhealthy and ambiguous relationship with number two.

When I entered the Army 1 July 72, the hospital at Redstone Arsenal in Huntsville was on a flat area on top of a hill. Officer housing started at the bottom of the hill and progressed according to rank up the hill. There was one house next to the hospital at the top of the hill. The houses lowest on the hill were for lieutenants, above those were houses for captains, above those were houses for majors (which I was), above those were houses for lieutenant colonels, then colonels, and the top of the hill on the same level as the hospital was a larger house saved for a general. I made a simple suggestion that since I was the only surgeon there on base at that time it would be nice to be able to walk across to the hospital from that house. The only problem was that I was only a lowly major. However, my reasoning was good. With much reluctance, the powers in charge of housing finally gave me permission to have the large single-family house within fifty yards of the hospital since I was always on call.

Within the first four to six weeks of being on post, the Army required that that you must put on a dress blue uniform and white gloves and visit the commanding general at his home on post. You were to appear at 1600 hours and stay there until 1615 hours. The only things I have maintained over the years since being in the Army are keeping time in 24 hours not 12 and writing dates, e.g. 30 June 74, my ETS or estimated time of separation, and my birthday 27 Dec 42. These habits help keep from making mistakes or misreading other's handwriting. At the commanding general's residence you were to leave your white gloves on the front table on a silver tray and mingle for fifteen minutes with the general and his friends. I did not want to do that! The required dress blue uniform cost $400 and I needed an air conditioning window unit for the house I was living in. I found myself needing to get out of going to a required function with the commanding general of the Army at Red Stone Arsenal. My problem was alleviated on meeting a young lieutenant who happened to take care of managing the daily schedule and social calendar for the general. I did a hemorrhoidectomy on the lieutenant. He was so pleased that on a postoperative visit to the office, he made a proposal I could not turn down. He asked if I would like to be moved from the "need to go to the general's party" list to the "already has been to the general's party" list. I quickly agreed. My problem was solved.

According to the paperwork I received, I was to become a major when I entered active duty in the United States Army. I had been credited for nine years of service for pay purposes, four years for medical school, one year for my internship, and four years for my surgical training. I was told that a major was an O4 or the first field grade officer. I didn't know what that meant, but I found out that the only way to be a part of the Army was as a major or above. One minor difference was the bill of your hat. This bill did not have to be polished as the one I had in college did. This one had some type of felt on it and there were "scrambled eggs" on the bill.

Since I arrived at the Army base on 1 July 72, I was the only physician there. Being the first to arrive, I was made chief of Professional Services, chief of Surgery, and chief of General Surgery. At the time I didn't realize how important this was to become.

I was one of the older hippie generation doctors and my hair was shoulder length. I was told to get a haircut and report to the commander of the hospital to be inspected. After the third haircut, he still did not approve and I was ordered to go to Building 1430. When I did, I found that it was a US Army barbershop. They had been notified that I was on my way and when I walked in, I was escorted to a barber chair and had a haircut with "white sidewalls," or extremely short hair around the ears. The only way I could retaliate was by not having my hair cut for the next six months.

I must have driven the commander of the hospital crazy. As a resident in training, I had to present each surgical case I wanted to do to my chief resident or attending physician. When I started in the Army I did the same thing. I would go to the commander's office and present my cases to him to get his approval for surgery. He said, "I don't care what you do. Don't bother me." This was my first introduction to the real practice of medicine.

Being chief of Professional Services, I obtained several privileges given only because I was the first doctor to show up on post. When the second surgeon arrived in August after six weeks of basic training, we both wanted to be off on Friday afternoon. I thought I was in trouble. You know that many doctors take an afternoon off during the week usually as an excuse to play golf. I went to the commander of the hospital and explained that the other surgeon and I both wanted Friday afternoon off. "So what's your problem?" the colonel asked. "I figured you would make that decision, sir." He replied, "No, that's the chief of Surgery's decision." So I told the other surgeon, "I'm sorry, but the chief of Surgery decided that Friday afternoon is mine." He was understandably mad but his screaming was to no avail. The chief of Surgery (me) had made the decision and he knew and recognized the protocol.

As an introduction to the US Army, we all had to go down to the enlisted training area to participate in a racial awareness program, better known as a RAP course. Both enlisted men and officers went together. There was a sergeant major, the top enlisted rank in the US Army, included in our group. I later found out that sergeant majors moved the Army. No one in the entire Army knew better how to take care of any situation whether for themselves or their commanders. Our group of eight sat around a conference table for this discussion. Many nationalities and colors were represented. They asked us how we wanted to be recognized and suggested that we use our first names. I, of course, went by my first name as did most of the rest of the people there. The sergeant major used his usual name, Sergeant Major. I also told our group of eight that if the Army ever centralized our RAP program, it would become the centralized racial awareness program and have the acronym CRAP course. No one laughed and I don't think this was ever considered as a suggestion to be pursued.

I knew that it was required that you return a salute from an enlisted man, especially when you were in an enlisted area. The enlisted man would stand at attention with the salute until an officer returned the salute. I found that if I just pushed my glasses up quickly with my right hand it was assumed to be a salute. This maneuver got me off the hook many times. It was an inappropriate salute, but at least I didn't leave an enlisted man standing at attention without a return salute.

Late one afternoon I was walking through the parking lot going to the PX, or base exchange store, to shop. Prices there were deeply discounted on most of the products they displayed from all over the world. Maybe that's where the idea for Walmart came about. TAPS was played at 17:00 hours every afternoon. All Army personnel over the entire post were supposed to stop, stand at attention, and salute the flag. Not knowing this, I kept walking. I thought it was unusual that I could walk directly into the store while everyone else stood in the parking lot. An Army officer stopped me and said, "You do not know what's going on, do you?" I told him that I had no idea what was happening. He said, "Every afternoon when TAPS is played, you must stand at attention and salute the flag until TAPS is finished." He also very cynically said, "You are not real Army anyway, are you?" Again in my usual blunt fashion, I replied, "No, I am not real Army, I'm unreal Army." I then turned and walked away not waiting for a reaction. I think this fact was substantiated by the obvious condition of my uniform. I never found out until a year after I was in the Army that my belt buckle was covered with a coat of shellac. The shellac should've been removed and then brass polish used regularly to keep the buckle shiny. Thank God there were US military men's corfam shoes issued to us. You didn't have to spit-polish them.

I worked with several of the dentists while I was in the Army and now am the proud possessor of eight gold caps which have lasted with no problems for over forty years since I've been out of the Army. I received excellent dental care there. The dentist that I originally saw in the dental clinic needed a vasectomy, so we traded services. I did a vasectomy on him and he gave me eight gold crowns over the two years I was there. He got good practice on my mouth and I was able to provide a service that both he and his wife wanted.

The physician who had been chief of Professional Services and chief of Surgery before me was an orthopedic surgeon. He eventually ended up in Spartanburg, South Carolina. While he and I were there for the first few weeks we shared his office. He had a large 50-gallon freshwater fish tank in his office. I never asked any questions about it and when he left he said, "Since this is going to be your office, you can keep the fish tank." I agreed without even thinking about it. I continued to take care of all the fish and equipment for the first year or so. One morning about 0700 hrs., the CID or Criminal Investigative Department of the Army came to my office. The officer said as he pointed, "Who's fish tank is that?" I responded that I did not know but it was in my office because it was in the office of the orthopedic surgeon who was there before me. The officer explained that the property officer from the veterinarian's office on post had lost track of the fish tank. The veterinarian on post actually did very little work except for grading the meat that came on post and some small animal work. But the fish tank belonged to the veterinarian department. The CID emptied the tank, flushed the fish, and took everything away. They put the empty equipment back in the veterinarian's office. Later in my practice in Jamestown, Tennessee, I was able to have a large 50-gallon saltwater aquarium. It gave hours of enjoyment for me and my staff as well as patients and children who came in my office. Since they never found out about it, the CID never gave me a problem.

I had my first encounter with attempting to fire one of the civilian personnel while in the Army. One of the lower-grade civilian typists wore a T-shirt to work in the clinic with F... (except the word was spelled out) across the front of the T-shirt in all capital letters. I asked her not to wear the shirt in front of my patients. She refused. Her response was, "Try to fire me." I stated that I would. I probably was not the first to try. Over the next two years, all my attempts were futile and she continued wearing the obnoxious T-shirt any time she wanted. I never understood how a government employee seemed to get away with things which would have immediately gotten her fired in the real world.

The United States Army had a protocol for answering the telephone. In surgery the person in charge usually answered the phone by saying, "Specialist Fourth Class Jones speaking, sir. How may I help you?" The Army required that the phone be answered the same way all over the entire post. I made a point that anytime I answered the phone I would say, "Joe's Bar and Grill, may I help you, sir?" To vary my routine on occasion, I would answer, "Joe's morgue—you stab 'em, we slab 'em. How can I help you, sir?" No one ever made remarks about my phone answering or reported me, at least that I was aware of. When I left the Army, my secretary at the clinic had a ceramic mug made for me. The mug had a doctor with long hair wearing a white coat and standing behind a bar with the words coming out of his mouth "Joe's Bar and Grill." I guess it was my "Purple Heart" for taking a shot for the troops.

Huntsville, Alabama, flourished due to Redstone Arsenal being a large base both physically and with the number of retirees who lived in the area. The hospital was quite busy. I found a friend no one of my patients who had gallbladder disease with gallstones, requiring one of my favorite operations. I saw this individual in the clinic next to the hospital. He was a GS 17 which was a very high-ranking government worker in both rank and pay in the civilian forces. I performed the operation for his severe gallbladder disease and he did quite well. When he got out of the hospital, he came to my clinic for his first postoperative visit. He asked, "Do you have any tools?" I replied, "Very few. I don't do a lot of work on things requiring tools outside surgery. Why do you ask?" And he casually remarked, "No reason really." The next morning I had a quite extensive set of tools in a metal toolbox on my back porch. I saw him the next week in the office and thanked him for the tools. He said, "What are you talking about? I don't know what you mean." I realized very quickly that such favors could not be granted, at least openly, while in the Army. Within the next year I operated on his granddaughter and on a postoperative visit, he showed up with his granddaughter and asked, "Do you have any metric tools?" and I again said, "No, I don't." And within the next week, I had a full set of metric tools mysteriously appear on my back porch. I had learned by then I could never thank him openly. He was happy to have the opportunity to provide me with government surplus.

It was in Alabama that I had reaffirmation of a statement I had heard many years earlier in Tennessee. I was on my way to Arab, Alabama. I was looking for the Joe V Clayton Chevrolet dealership. Corvette allotments for dealerships were made on the number of pickup trucks sold. I had heard that there were twenty five Corvettes sitting on the lot because that dealership sold more pickup trucks than any other dealership in the entire state. I was driving on my way out of Huntsville which at that time was surrounded by a lot of farmland. I really had no idea where the dealership was and I didn't have a map with me. I stopped when I saw a farmer close to the side of the road and asked him where Arab (pronounced A-rab) was. I told him I was looking for the Joe V Clayton Chevrolet dealership because I wanted to look at the Corvettes. He slowly stopped, leaned on his shovel, and replied, "I don't think you can get there from here."

Since I was one of the first fully trained surgeons that the Army had had on base in several years at Redstone Arsenal, it became quite obvious a lot of surgery had backed up and suddenly appeared. One of the first patients I saw was a newborn male whose parents wanted him circumcised. The Jewish father told me that, according to tradition, his son needed to be circumcised on the eighth day which was the coming Friday. He asked me to do it in the recovery room with nothing but local anesthesia for the child. While the rabbi and father carried out the prescribed traditions, I had a nurse help me while I circumcised the baby. Of course, even with local anesthesia, the little boy was yelling and screaming. All the while during the procedure, the rabbi and father were exchanging one Army hat for one yarmulke, reading scriptures, and drinking wine. When everything was over, several things happened. Both the father and rabbi were happy, the baby stopped crying, and I received the remainder of the bottle of wine. After the word got out, there was a plethora of circumcisions to do.

During the first few weeks in the Army, there were many social gatherings to get all the new physicians and families introduced to each other. Number two and I had a lot of difficulty keeping all the lies straight as to dates of marriage (we were not married yet) and where the kids were all the time. Secrets that were difficult to keep. Sir Walter Scott said, "O, what a tangled web we weave when first we practice to deceive."

After the first year on post, we had a full complement of eight physicians in the fifty-bed hospital. We all did some night work "moonlighting" in a local clinic in Huntsville that took care of indigent people. Most were patients who could not see the physicians in town because they had no money or insurance. After working at this clinic for approximately three months, the dreaded CID raided the clinic when they found that it was being staffed by Army physicians. We were receiving pay from the government for being in the Army and the clinic was receiving pay from the government. The clinic in turn paid us for working there. The CID considered that this was illegal and we were all accused of "double dipping." It made no sense to any of us. The CID had confiscated a call schedule from one of the doctor's homes. They then appeared at the office of each one of the four physicians on post and threatened to reprimand each of us with an article 15. This could demote us to a lower rank, or cause us a dishonorable discharge according to AR 40–5 paragraphs 1 through 5. The hospital commander decided that we could compromise. If we all apologized, the Army would forgive us and this "incident" would not become a part of our permanent records. I was very upset about the whole process and refused to apologize because we were helping indigent patients who needed care. After speaking with the commander of the hospital, I prepared a very sarcastic, tersely written note that explained exactly how I felt. I said, "Please forgive me, for I have sinned and come short of the expectations of the Army." It was accepted and nothing else was ever said. There was no record of it ever having happened.

I learned what the initials GI really stood for- "government issue." While taking care of patients, I had a young captain come into my office. He had had several episodes of sigmoid diverticulitis. It was obvious he was going to need surgery consisting of removing the left side of his colon because of the continuing abscesses and disease. After much thought about the situation, he said, "I have been in the Army for eleven years and just re-upped for four more years. I'm going to retire in the Army. I think I'll just try to control everything with diet and see if we can avoid surgery." It was possible to do this, but it was more likely he was going to require surgery to have a planned removal of part of his colon. This could also prevent the possibility of a colostomy in the future. He came back to my office and said he was going to take his chances by being treated medically without surgery. When the commander of the hospital found out that this GI wanted to delay his surgery, he intervened and gave the captain a couple of options: he could either have the surgery done by me there at the hospital or he could leave the Army. That's when I found out the true meaning of government issue. The captain decided to stay with me and had his surgery performed. He did well after the surgery; however, it was not what he had wanted to do from the very beginning.

The surgeon who I was to replace had only about six months before he was to leave the Army. He was really interested in ENT (Ear, Nose, Throat) surgery and had only one year of surgical training. He did a lot of surgery that he probably shouldn't have because no one, including the commander of the hospital, would ever tell him what to do or not to do. My first knowledge of this surgeon came from when he was in a crowded afternoon surgical clinic. He was in his office and had patients waiting to be seen. An E 6 Sergeant was also sitting in his office as a patient. In full view of the E 6, this surgeon urinated in the sink of his office, climbed out the window, and disappeared. He later admitted to me that he had done this. I was called into the commander's office within the next week and we discussed this incident. I realized that one of the other benefits of being chief of Surgery was that the surgeon was now my problem. I had to keep him out of trouble with himself and others.

Another reason that surgeon got away with what he did was the fantastic job the Army did on brainwashing the enlisted men, retirees, and dependents. They thought Army doctors could transplant heads in the clinic under local anesthesia or at least walk on water. The ENT doctor had been doing vasectomies (a sterilization procedure on a man) in the clinic under local anesthesia. After arriving on post, I realized there was a problem. The sergeant, who had been sitting in the surgeon's office and saw the surgeon crawl out the window, had come back from temporary duty. He had had a vasectomy done three month earlier by this surgeon. When he arrived home he found his wife was pregnant. I knew we had a real problem. The sergeant started asking me and others questions about the surgeon. He wanted to know what the surgeon's schedule was, when was he leaving the Army, and how could he get in touch with the doctor. On further questioning, I found out that the vasectomy had been done in the office. The sergeant wanted to talk to the doctor about his surgery. I checked with the commander of the hospital and found that the surgeon was leaving within the next two weeks and when I told the sergeant about this, he became very agitated. The full story came out.

He told me that he had come to the office for a vasectomy. His wife had asked him to have the vasectomy done because they had three children and she thought he could recover while he was on temporary duty or TDY for three months. After coming home and finding his wife was pregnant, he said, "I wanted to kill my wife. Then I found out the possibility existed that I could be the father." After having a sperm count done and motile sperm found, it was obvious that one of the sergeant's vas had not been tied off. He then transferred all his frustration and anger toward the physician who had done the vasectomy. Since he couldn't sue the doctor to have him help support the child, he wanted to do bodily harm to him. With the quick thinking of the hospital commander, the decision was made to allow the offending doctor to leave base early by an alternate exit point. He was gone before the sergeant found out where he was.

I had to perform a repeat vasectomy on the sergeant (and five other men who the surgeon had done earlier in his office) in surgery under general anesthesia. I continued doing vasectomies in surgery under general anesthesia for the next two years while I was in the Army to gain back everyone's confidence. They became the first six of about six hundred vasectomies that I did in the next two years. This must have been a Guinness record in the Army at least according to the pathologist we used in Atlanta to check each vas I removed. Most were done on Friday morning on an outpatient basis. They were admitted Friday morning, put to sleep for about ten minutes while I did the surgery, and then awakened and sent home. This was the first surgical outpatient program that I had ever heard about and participated in.

The same partially trained surgeon also had done a bilateral adrenalectomy just before I got there. This is a difficult and lengthy surgery. It was performed on a female patient for a solitary metastasis of breast cancer to her femur. I had performed only one of these procedures over my four years of surgical training. This surgeon said he had read about the operation and wanted to do one. And he did it. When I took over care of the patient, she had several severe complications. The adrenals were producing estrogen which was stimulating the metastatic disease. By removing the stimulation of the hormones from the adrenals, the size of the tumor in her femur should decrease. But she almost died. Doing the surgery was the easier part. Taking care of the patient before and after the surgery was more difficult. The mineralocorticoids which the adrenals produce were not replaced. I had to replace these, remove clots from her legs, and give special medications before she finally recovered about six weeks later. I still have the St. Christopher's money clip the patient and her husband gave me. Two years later when I left the Army, she was still in good health and free of metastasis. Coincidence or miracle? The surgeon was poorly prepared and should never even have attempted to perform the surgery. My first encounter with medical malpractice.

In 1973 a tornado came through Huntsville and caused quite a bit of damage. Several school buses on post were overturned. Roofs were taken off buildings. About 1700 that day most of the doctors on the Army base were called downtown to Huntsville General Hospital to help with the injured. The tornado winds were so high they had actually pushed an intact piece of straw through a 1" by 4" section of barn wood. While I was in the Emergency Room, I was presented with a patient who had perforated a duodenal ulcer caused by the stress of and not a direct injury from the tornado. This was before there were medications to decrease or block the acidity in the stomach. I had to take him to surgery as an emergency. I remember distinctly having one of the local policeman run in, leave the doors of the emergency room open, and scream, "Hit the deck!" I got under the closest thing there, which was the stretcher that my patient was lying on. We could hear what sounded like a freight train as the tornado went across the hospital. That night I took the patient to surgery and repaired a perforated ulcer, turned his care over to another surgeon there, walked out of the hospital, and never saw the patient again.

One of the first friends I made while in the Army was a radiologist from Chicago. We both enjoyed our stay there and did quite a lot of work together. But sometimes both of us were difficult to handle especially if we were together. Though we came from different parts of the United States, we both received similar instructions from our mothers, "You have to watch those folks from down South," from his mother and "You have to watch those folks from up North" from my mother. He said that when he found out he was going to Huntsville, Alabama, his mother told him, "As you drive down from Illinois into Kentucky and Tennessee, you have to roll the windows of the car up and lock the doors." I replied, "That's amazing because I was told the same story except in the reverse order." My mother had said, "When you leave Tennessee and Kentucky, you have to roll up the car windows and lock the doors." We became fast friends. When we were told to have official pictures made for the Army, we both refused. We were very busy and didn't want have our work interrupted. However, we both received a direct order. We were to be at the base photographer's office at 1630 Friday. We were both to be dressed in our winter green uniforms and hats. We both appeared and got our "official portraits" taken, but before we left we asked the photographer for a favor. He reluctantly agreed. We both unbuttoned the top couple of buttons in our uniform coats, put cigars in our mouths, pushed back the Army hat with braid to the back of our heads, put our thumbs in our unbuttoned lapels, and had our official Army photographs made. Since we both outranked the photographer and didn't want to get him in trouble, we gave him a direct order to cover his doing this favor. We all laughed.

I had an interesting time with my family while in the Army. Regulations stated that you could not take children unattended into the commissary unless they were twelve years old or had their own ID cards.

Since I did not have custody of the kids, I could not get ID's for them. All four were under seven years of age. When we went grocery shopping, I had to place all four in two grocery carts or "buggies" and then push another buggy around to put in groceries. They even had personnel there to check ID's or help place kids in the grocery carts.

At least the movies and snacks were cheap. One night after a late movie we got home and I found we were locked out of the house. I stood my five-year-old son on my shoulders and had him go through the bathroom window and crawl into a dark house. The neighbors could hear him yelling the whole time he was running through the house to get to the back door to unlock it so everybody could get in. A second son was three years old and would get up at 0200 or 0300 in the morning and play with toys in his room. He would also unlock the back door to go outside to play. I had to install a dead bolt on the door to prevent his going out in the dark. My third son was just over one year old. He would tear his disposable diaper into small pieces and throw them out of his playpen. He would also pull toilet paper in one long piece throughout the house. By being part of a large family, everyone was used to very little time for modesty. My third son also attempted to collect a "midstream clean catch urine" by sticking his hand into the stream while standing next to me and watching as I urinated.

Many happy times were spent with my children there. Most of my other time was spent alone or at work. Number two developed friendships that caused great concern, especially with an OB/GYN physician from Atlanta that did her "routine" physical exams. Even the happiness from the children did not improve the condition of our marriage. As stated above, we were not married until six weeks after entering the Army. We lied to everyone about us being married and having four children. Then a divorce 23 Feb 73 and remarriage 19 March 73. Times with number two were surreal. I got my coins back with the condition I would sell them there in Huntsville at a local coin shop. I did but have regretted it many times. Things were on and off but mostly off with number two. My first concern was my kids.

One afternoon I was called in to the office of the commander of the hospital and was told that President Richard Nixon was coming to a political fundraiser in town. I was to be his personal surgeon should anything happened to him during his time in Huntsville. I responded to the hospital commander that Friday afternoon was my afternoon off and I was going back to Chattanooga to be with my children. He said, "No!" He needed me to stay in Huntsville. I was to follow President Nixon around everywhere he went, and God forbid, if anything happened that required him to have surgery, I was going to have to do it. Again I said, "Thanks, I'm not interested in doing that. I'm not a political person. I'm going to Chattanooga." Again, I found out what a direct order was. Like with the haircuts and photographs. I was directly ordered to remain on the Army base in Huntsville that Friday and to be close to President Nixon the entire time he was in Huntsville. It was necessary for me to follow the minor motorcade and physically be there until President Nixon flew out that night. I did this against my will but I had no option but to follow a direct order. The next day I complained to the hospital commander. I told him that I had done a favor for President Nixon and the two physicians who traveled with him. One of them was a cardiologist and one was proctologist. I knew that no one would believe that anything like this had happened to me. As proof that I had been President Nixon's surgeon, I wanted a letter from each of the two doctors and an autographed first-day cover from the White House. Approximately six to eight weeks later, I received two signed letters from the doctors and they signed a first-day cover along with President Nixon. These are framed and now hang in my office as one of the things I am most proud of and as a symbol of my service to my country. Come by, I'll show them to you.

I also had the opportunity to meet Buford Pusser, the person about whom the movie *Walking Tall* was written, and personally get his autograph. He was killed about two years later by the criminals he had fought. I got to meet George Wallace, the governor of Alabama. He wrote a nice note to me:

"To Dr. Carroll,
Best Wishes,
George Wallace, Governor of Alabama."

While in the Army, I had a sign over the entrance to my office show-ing my name and a Bard Parker scalpel with blood dripping from its tip and a pool of blood below it. It's also here in my office.

I had not had my hair cut for quite some time after my initial encoun-ter with the Army barber. I wore a Mickey Mouse Timex watch which I called my official Army watch. My hair, unpolished belt buckle, Mickey Mouse watch, and office sign occasionally caused some problems. I had a full colonel come to my office, take a look at me, up and down, from hair to belt buckle to my watch. He turned around and left the office, only to come back a couple of minutes later, cursing. He said, "You are the only one here! I guess I'll have to see you." I may not have looked the part of a "real Army doctor," but I gave good service and got excellent surgical results for the two years I was in the Army.

I found that the chief of Professional Services also had many respon-sibilities in the Army. This became important as much accumulated information was presented to me, including the yearly budget. I had to approve certain parts of the budget that concerned the equipment we used in surgery and in the clinic. Before the due date to turn in our final budget, I worked hard to save as much money as possible. I succeeded but was approached by the commander of the hospital who said, "You don't understand. If you undercut your budget by ten percent, our budget will be ten percent less next year and you may need it then. You'll have to buy something you want so we will come in just above the budget." Having an extra $10,000 that first year, I bought an esophagogastroduo-denoscope and a colonoscope. I had never used either, but knew I had a captive audience. Having both of these scopes to use, I learned to do EGDs and C-scopes on the patients who needed them. I did over one hundred of these procedures during the last year I was in the Army. On entering private practice in Chattanooga after leaving the Army, I had a problem. It was uncommon for general surgeons to be granted privileges for EGDs and C-scopes. When I presented my cases, the hospitals would not allow me privileges to do them unless I had a preceptor or gastroenterologist who would watch me do the procedures. I asked a friend who was a gastroenterologist to help me. He was amazed that I had such good manual dexterity and hand-eye coordination. He quickly conceded that I could do the procedures as well as he could after two years of residency and training in gastroenterology. I was permitted to use the scopes and made this a part of my private practice. I later taught surgical residents at Erlanger how to do both procedures.

On leaving the Army, I found another problem with regulations. I supposedly was in charge of having my grass cut every two weeks. In reality the personnel who mowed the grass around the hospital would come over to my lodging and cut the approximately two acres of grass. While I was signing out, I was asked if I had mowed the grass within the week prior to leaving. I said, "No", since I had never cut the grass. I was told that there was a requirement and regulation that on leaving, the grass had to be mowed. I responded to the enlisted man that this was impossible since I had never done this and I did not have a lawnmower. Trying to be helpful, he said, "Hey, Doc: an officer's word is accepted as the truth." Being rather slow in understanding what was going on, he repeated that statement to me and told me again that an officer's word was accepted as the truth. I then understood what he was getting at and told him, "The grass is in great shape and has been cut." He took my word and I was allowed to sign out. The house was checked back in to be given to the next waiting lucky recipient, probably a general.

One of the requirements during my residency in general surgery was to write a scientific article to be published in a medical journal. I did the work and the article was published in the *Journal of Pediatric Surgery* in February 1973. It was titled, " Absence of Musculature of the Distal Ileum: A Cause of Neonatal Intestinal Obstruction." I always thought I would continue training to become a pediatric surgeon. I had gotten Dr. Reisman to help me attend the first annual meeting of pediatric surgeons in Bermuda when I was a resident. He even got the hospital to cover the cost of my attending. I think I was the first general surgery resident in Chattanooga to travel outside the Continental United States for a continuing medical education program. I had been on a tour of the Northeast to the pediatric surgery training programs. I had visited Baltimore, Maryland and Johns Hopkins. In Philadelphia, Pennsylvania, I talked about a pediatric surgery residency with Dr. C. Everett Koop (his friends called him Chick), who later became Surgeon General of the United States. I also visited Boston, Massachusetts, and Toronto, Canada, both of which had excellent programs in pediatric surgery. I had spoken to one of the surgeons practicing in Chattanooga who had finished a residency at Johns Hopkins University. He had written a letter to Dr. Alex Haller who was in charge of pediatric surgery at Johns Hopkins. I had been accepted to begin a residency there in pediatric surgery after I finished my time in the Army.

As the time approached for my ETS, estimated time of separation, from the Army, I had a big decision to make. I always said I didn't want to be separated from the Army, I actually wanted a divorce. The Army always said that they could call you back into service at any time up to age fifty. I knew that if I were to spend two extra years in training for pediatric surgery, I would then want to continue with pediatric cardiovascular surgery. That would require two more years of training that would likely take place in New York City. This would be an extra four years of training and would require living in a very large metropolitan area to have a viable pediatric surgery practice. Since all four of my children were under nine years of age at the time I finished my service in the Army, I knew that the additional four years of training and the necessity of my practicing in large city would probably separate me from my children forever. I finally decided that my children were more important than my career. I turned down the residency in pediatric surgery.

I then had an offer to practice surgery in a small county hospital in Northeast Alabama where I had been "moonlighting." It was a very rural area. The hospital offered me $100,000 to come there with my family and practice general surgery. Again I had a gigantic decision to make. Because of the difficulties with number two and not wanting to leave my family, I decided to start work in Chattanooga and join a partnership with my old chief of surgery and another general surgeon at a salary of $25,000 a year. Was it a missed opportunity or a good decision? It for sure was not a coincidence. Number two was of no help with any of these decisions.

CHAPTER 12

I moved back to Chattanooga, Tennessee, in June 1974 after finishing my two years of active duty in the Army. I was commissioned in the Army as a major when I arrived at Redstone Arsenal but was promoted to lieutenant colonel by staying in the reserves.

The move back to Chattanooga was uneventful. In order to buy a house in an older section of North Chattanooga, I had to sell my prized collection of United States revenue stamps. This was a suggestion made by number two. In actuality it was more of a demand. The $18,000 received for my collection became a down payment on a nice older house that needed a lot of work. By the time I started work in July 1974, number two had made her $10,000 arrangement (unknown to me at that time) with number one and finally the children began staying with us all the time. Number one had remarried and moved to Alabama. After several visits with the kids at her new home, she decided that she didn't particularly want four kids in her new relationship. This was related to me by the kids. The paperwork for the adoption of my children by number two was completed and became official. She even had the birth certificates changed to have her name on them as mother of my kids.

Number two was adamant about having another child. I had had a vasectomy done in Chattanooga as a resident in December 1971 and I could no longer father children. Number two had given up one baby for adoption and lost a second by miscarriage, abortion, or adoption, and now demanded another child. In order to keep her as stable as possible, it was necessary for me to agree to a reanastomosis of my vasectomy, which was performed in California in 1973. It was not successful and the second reanastomosis was performed in New York City in 1974.

After these changes, number two felt all the kids, including any additional ones, had to be enrolled in private schools. The fees for the Bright School, a private elementary school, took a large part of my initial salary. My daughter was able to attend Girl's Preparatory School in the seventh grade with an associated jump in tuition. My three sons were eventually enrolled in Baylor School as they entered the seventh grade. My salary increased over time but it was extremely difficult to pay for everyone attending private schools. As you would imagine, finances became a part of the difficulties of my life. After number two officially adopted my four children, her life became focused on having another child. After the second surgery for the reanastomosis of my vas, she became pregnant and my last son Peter was born in July 1977. Her relationship with the first four children became more intense and began to change.

After several renovations of our first old house and after the birth of Peter, it was necessary to find another residence in order to give all of us adequate room. Number two did not approve of any of my choices of other houses. This became another of many points of contention between us. The few years of the late 70s and early 80s became unbearable. I continued with summer camp in the Army to provide extra income and maintain my rank in the United States Army. My final attempt to make what I considered correct decisions and stand on my own for myself and my family brought about a very bitter, long, and expensive divorce which culminated in my "drug situation." I believe machinations by number two were intricately woven through these years.

My children helped me maintain my sanity. At nighttime, around the dinner table, it was not unusual for them to ask and for me to tell them some of the gorier and more flamboyant aspects of surgery. One of the cases I told them was about a young boy who jumped on a motorcycle behind his friend. As they rode down the back side of Missionary

Ridge, they missed the curve at the bottom of the hill and went through a picket fence in front of a house. The driver did not get a scratch but his friend behind him had a 1" by 4" piece of the white picket fence go through his neck. Even with an attempted tracheotomy at the scene, the boy died. I told the details of patients who came in the ER with grotesque injuries that had occurred to them and included the surgery I performed on many of them. The kids became used to hearing such conversations at the dinner table so it never interfered with their eating. My thinking and storytelling was correctly critiqued when my oldest son asked, "Dad, do any of your patients ever live?" After that I tried to make it a practice to include simpler cases where the survival rate was much better and where events were not so dramatic. We also discussed more important subjects like whether Armando's or George's had the best hamburgers or fried chicken livers in town. I loved the hamburgers at Armando's but all of them liked the fried chicken livers at George's.

One of the best things I ever started with my children after we moved was what I called "Happy Time." I would shrilly whistle and everyone would gather in the family room before bedtime. Each of the children was required to tell of at least one event during their day that caused them to be happy. Everybody was required to participate. Sometimes their happy time involved talking to a friend or teacher, a test grade, an achievement, or just that the entire day had been a good day. When number two was pregnant, she was to deliver on the birthday of my third son. That evening before bedtime, he stated, "My happy time is that my brother was not born on my birthday!" All of us laughed and agreed that it's important to have your birthday reserved just for your own celebration.

I always tried to be honest with my kids. At Christmas time they would ask, "Daddy, is there a real Santa Claus?" I would always reply, "No, it's me! I am the one that buys all your Christmas gifts." I was always greeted with a chorus of, "No you're not!" At least I told them the truth.

After my fourth son was born, one of his favorite things as a child was to ask me to tell him a story. In fact all of the kids enjoyed this. I think storytelling came naturally to me because of my dad being a minister and my mother answering any question and taking 10 minutes or more to do it. Peter would ask me many times, "Daddy, tell me a story about when you were a little boy," or "Daddy, did they have cars when you were a little boy?" He and the other kids restored both my faith and my ability to relate stories of my past.

I slowly developed a real love for real estate. I spent many late nights watching TV and listening to and buying several "Nothing Down" real estate courses. One of the best friends I had was a real estate broker who mentored me and helped with most of my buying and selling. She was able to assist me and helped me get my real estate license. She had more common sense than most people. All of this led to my children's involvement. I bought an old commercial building in downtown Chattanooga and explained to the kids what we wanted to accomplish. Together we would go to the building and take down the partitions and insides of the building. They learned what renovation was and why we did it, to increase the return on our investment. We actually went into the basement of the old building and found an entrance to a completely lower level which had been the original street level years before. The drainage system was eight feet in diameter and ran down the middle of and underneath Broad Street toward the river. Our building was on the corner of 8th Street and Broad Street. On the lower level, we could actually see sidewalks and debris from the past. We lovingly called this area "Underground Chattanooga." I have in my office now an old bottle that we found on the street approximately ten feet below the present Broad Street. The bottle is embossed, "The Stone Fizz of America, 6 fl. oz., and CHATT." It brings back fond memories.

The kids learned about rental property. At one point I had real estate holdings worth over $2 million and was able to pay no federal income tax for two years. We all learned about politics as the US House and Senate changed all the rules concerning mortgage interest deductions. I was forced to sell all the rental property that I had but maintained the commercial properties. Another purchase was a downtown commercial building with a 6 foot tall by 12 foot wide semicircular stained glass window in the upper portion of the building on Market Street, the main street downtown. We eventually had fluorescent lights placed behind the window. The kids loved to drive by at night and see that window lighted. The majority of my real estate holdings were lost in the divorce to number two who promptly sold all the properties she was given.

Another of my best friends owned a stainless steel company and the two of us would meet every Friday morning at Shoney's in downtown Chattanooga for breakfast. We had our "mind group" and would talk about anything and everything, especially real estate. We went to church together and at one time we were both listed in the top one hundred fifty "movers and shakers" of Chattanooga. He was much higher up the list than I. He stuck closer than a brother through my divorce and helped financially and otherwise through the drug fiasco and is still a good friend.

While in the Army I became good friends with a man who made stained glass windows for churches and homes. I began doing some glass cutting and window and lamp making on my own. In Chattanooga we noticed a lot of stained glass windows that no one took care of or appreciated. Many of them were broken. I made it a game with the kids to drive around Chattanooga and see who could find the most stained glass windows. I would then go to the owners of the property and ask them if they would like a new plate glass window in place of the dirty, darkened and usually covered stained glass. I found that most people preferred the extra light that new clear windows gave. I developed a nice collection of stained glass by doing this.

There was an Elks Club that had been located on the fourth floor of a building just across from the Courthouse downtown. I arranged with the city to remove the Elks Club stained glass windows covered with years of grime. We would go downtown at night to remove the windows and replace them with plate glass. It was dirty work but well worth it even though sometimes we were so black and dirty that we would be refused service at the Krystal hamburger franchise on 6th Street, a block away.

Our work was stopped and I didn't understand why. The city decided that since the windows were on the fourth floor, it was too dangerous for me to replace them, especially with kids around. A decision was made that they would remove the windows, replace them, and bring the stained glass to my home. I was really very appreciative. I got a beautiful set of windows and didn't have to do the physical work to remove them. I had the only bathroom in Chattanooga with a large backlighted stained glass antlered elk behind the commode.

My daughter wanted to apply for work at a Krystal hamburger franchise in North Chattanooga. She had done well in school and at her job interview was given a math problem. Her exam consisted of keeping track of the number of hamburgers, French fries, and Cokes that came in as an order, calculate the total cost, and then give the correct amount of change from a $20 bill. When she hesitated, the manager asked, "Don't you know the answer?" She replied, "Is that all of the problem." He nodded his head yes, she gave him the correct answer, and was immediately hired.

Since my finances were usually tight, I did not want to spend the $75 necessary to have our family dog spayed. I managed to obtain some injectable Ketamine to use as anesthesia for her. I had all the instruments ready for surgery after the dog had been injected. My second son was standing and intently watching. He looked me straight in the eye and said, "Dad, have you ever done one of these before?" I answered, "Yes, I do this on humans all the time." His response was, "Yeah, Dad. But this is our dog." I was able to make a lower midline abdominal incision, pull the uterus up, and remove it. The incision was sewn up in record time and I saved $75.

The difficulties in my marriage exaggerated inconsistencies in my spiritual life. On returning to Chattanooga, number two refused to attend the Church of God with me and the kids. We started attending the First Christian Church. I was able to serve on the Finance Committee and we became involved in the church. It was at this church that I got badly burned. I was telling ghost stories on Halloween at a kid's alternative service at church. A local plastic surgeon had told me that if I took a bowl of rock salt, poured medical alcohol over it and lighted it, it would burn with an eerily green light. He had supplied a one-liter metal can of alcohol from his office. I followed his advice and everything worked well as I read stories to the children who were there. I wanted to take my kids throughout the rest of the fun and games that the church had provided. I placed a ceramic top over the aluminum container I used for the salt and alcohol mixture. The fire when out immediately. I was away approximately 30 minutes. On returning, I took the top off the aluminum container and touched the sides. There was no warmth present but on pouring alcohol back across the salt, there was an explosion. The legs of my blue jeans were soaked with alcohol and caught on fire along with my socks. I had severe burns on both ankles and legs. I walked out of the church and drove myself to Erlanger Hospital. I was admitted and had skin grafts to my right thigh and both ankles. I had many visits with the Hubbard Tank and had to learn to walk again. I have a picture in my mind at the time of the accident seeing two adult men watching while I burned. They were too afraid to do anything. Number two brought in a sheet and covered my legs to eventually smother the fire. After several surgeries and skin grafts I was told that I would have permanent difficulties with my legs and walking. Twenty-two days later I walked out and drove home. I wore full-length Jobst compression stockings for another six weeks but I had a full recovery. Miracle or coincidence?

Number two decided we should try the First Baptist Church. The church was next-door to the YMCA and it was enjoyable to have the kids participate in many activities at church and then walk to the YMCA after Wednesday services. I developed several lifelong friends at the first Baptist Church. On a Christmas Eve, I had a friend from First Baptist give me a call. His daughter had dearly loved a horse for over thirty years. They had grown up together but now her horse was "down." It was my understanding that after this happened, a horse frequently would never get up again. He asked, after apologizing for calling on Christmas Eve, if I would come and help put the horse out of its misery. He could not do it on his own. I injected several vials of potassium chloride IV into the horse with no effect at all. His daughter could not stand the thought of shooting her beloved horse, so to keep things noiseless, it was necessary for me to perform a bilateral pneumothorax on the horse. This was one of the most unusual ways my family ever spent a Christmas Eve.

I used to take my kids to a farm owned by my friend's father-in-law. They were able to learn to drive a tractor and pull a "bush hog". I learned "bee keeping" and how to "rob" a hive for the honey. The kids learned how strawberries, corn, and potatoes grew. They also learned the value of hard work. We used to start early in the mornings, have a large lunch and a short nap before going back in the field to work again.

We remained at the first Baptist Church for quite some time. However, the Baptists have rules too. They were pleased to have me on the finance committee and accept my tithes, but I could never be a deacon. A deacon must be the husband of only one wife. Of course I questioned this, not because I wanted to be a deacon but because I did not believe in polygamy. In my opinion, I was the husband of only one wife. They explained that if I had ever been married before, I was the husband of more than one wife. I never understood this and still don't.

On one occasion the choir director at the Baptist Church had the choir sing a new song, "The KING Is Coming," written by Bill Gaither. After the choir finished the song, the congregation was so enthralled that everyone stood up and silently praised the Lord. Several weeks later the choir director wanted to have the choir perform the song again. This time, he said, "If y'all don't control yourselves and not overreact, we're not going to be able to sing it again!" In the Church of God, we called that "quenching the Spirit." I could no longer tolerate the Baptist Church. After our divorce, number two moved the children to the Presbyterian Church.

After returning to Chattanooga, one of the hospitals I admitted patients to was Erlanger. I spent one week out of every month working with the residents in trauma and helping with their surgical cases.

The residents and interns had continued the practice of having a Christmas party. Now that I was an attending surgeon, I was invited to attend and looked forward to going. To show the advances in technology, instead of having Santa Claus and his elves as we had done in the late 60s and early 70s, video was used. One of the funniest videos I've ever seen was shown at that party. The video was shot from the head of an examining table with a young doctor sitting between the legs of what appeared to be a pregnant patient lying on the table. The doctor who was supposed to be examining the patient stated that there was a new way to determine the sex of the baby prior to delivery. He put a glove under his chin, pulled the rest of the glove over his face, mask, and hair cover, and quickly disappeared between the patient's legs. I laughed until I cried.

In addition to Erlanger, I also regularly made rounds at Parkridge Hospital, Memorial Hospital, and Children's Hospital. It was at Parkridge Hospital that I encountered one of the most incompetent nurses I've ever seen and the only nurse I succeeded in getting fired. I had removed a large melanoma from the lower back of a patient and had a skin graft sutured over the surgical site. That evening she called me and said that on changing the dressing, the skin graft had come off. I told her that was impossible and I went to the hospital to check. She had removed all the sutures, changed the dressing and removed the skin graft thinking this was part of the dressing. I spoke to the CNO the next morning and eventually the nurse was fired.

I met a nurse there who made rounds with the attending physicians when they came to the surgical floor where she worked. While we were making rounds one morning, she asked me, "What kind of sex do you like?" I told her, "That's none of your business." But she persisted. She said, "I wear no makeup or perfume. When we get to an empty room I'll do whatever you want." I found out later that she made the same proposal to many of the attending doctors, some of whom accepted her offer.

Parkridge had a pathologist who was thought to be a homosexual. Before CT scans, studies showed that ten to fifteen percent of the appendices removed were normal and showed no pathology. I realized that all of the ones that I had removed at Parkridge had pathological findings. My percentage was one hundred percent positive. I knew I was good but not that good. I went to the pathologist's office to discuss this with him and he made a sexual offer to me. I told him I did not want to participate. Nothing was ever mentioned again, but after that my pathologic findings decreased to normal levels.

Even at thirty-four years of age I was still quite naïve. I met a young man by the name of Rod in surgery. He was the circulating nurse for my case that day. He had a lisp, one crossed eye, and acted very effeminate. I had asked for a certain instrument and he was slow in getting it for me. Trying to be funny, I said, in my usual blunt, surgical manner, "My God, Rod, are you queer?" You could have heard a pin drop. Evidently I was the last person to know, at least in the OR, that Rod was homosexual or "queer," the term common at that time. He laughed and said, "With a nickname like Rod, having a lisp, being cross-eyed, could I be anything else?" All the tension was broken and we all laughed. I became good friends with Rod. His partner was not monogamous. Rod approached me on another occasion and asked if he should be taking antibiotics while his partner went to an Atlanta "bath house." I first asked, "What is a bath house?" and then, "Are you afraid that he will be exposed to STDs from someone else?" If that was the case, then maybe he should be on antibiotics. Rod replied, "I'm not worried about him having relations with someone, but how many." I looked askance at Rod and he said, "He will have as many as thirty exposures over the weekend." My answer was, "He's more of a man than I am." Rod replied, "That depends on whether you're giving or receiving." I started him on antibiotics.

There was always a problem with doctors keeping up with their medical records. At Erlanger Hospital in my residency, it was easy enough to have the CEO hold our paychecks in his office until our medical records were completed. At Parkridge Hospital, I became aware of the difficulty with practicing physicians. If the attending physicians did not complete their medical records, the only threat the CEO could hold over their heads was that the doctor could not admit anyone to the hospital unless his medical records were completed. I heard doctors complain many times because they had surgery scheduled but the administrator held firm in saying that they could not admit people to the hospital or perform surgery until all their medical records were completed. In one way or the other, money always solved the problem.

I removed a malignant melanoma from behind a patient's right ear. The man was married and had three kids. He returned to my office rather reluctantly three months later with his wife who complained that her husband constantly smelled a dead rat. Many times early in the morning he would awaken his family to search the house for that "dead rat" smell. I began his workup which eventually showed metastatic melanoma to his brain. He died within the next three months.

Surgeons as a general rule are stable, but some are not. One that I frequently saw in the surgical lounge at Parkridge was rather obnoxious. I recognized him because he was several years ahead of me in the residency program at Erlanger Hospital. He would write his history and physical exam, his operative note, and his postoperative orders, all before he even walked in to begin the surgery. He would have patients lined up for block and a half outside his office. Later he was convicted of running a pain clinic where he sold narcotic prescriptions for $100 each and gave them to patients without ever examining them.

One patient who came to my office added special meaning to my life. She had had breast cancer in the past. As a hobby, she made ceramic Christmas trees with small multicolored plastic lights on the branches. All were lighted by a bulb inside the Christmas tree. She sold most of these trees for $35 each. She had a very aggressive cancer and eventually developed metastatic disease. One July afternoon she walked into my office and brought a beautiful white ceramic Christmas tree with various colored lights. She presented this to me. When I asked her, "What's the occasion? How much do I owe you?" She replied, "We're having Christmas in July!" As she gave me the gift, she made me promise that I would be with her when she passed away. I agreed. She knew her time was short. I admitted her to the hospital and within a few days, I got a call from the patient to come to her room. On arriving, she asked if I would sit with her for the next hour or so because she felt she was dying.

I held her hand and cried. I felt her spirit leave her and was able to fulfill my promise. I believe she went from a Christmas in July in Chattanooga, Tennessee, to heaven. Coincidence or miracle?

Due to my strict upbringing, I was never allowed to drink alcohol or smoke cigarettes. I'm sure my mother and father had always lived the same way. On one occasion we had a group of people at my house for a "family reunion." One of number two's aunts had prepared baked beans which I'm sure were baked with bourbon. My mother thought they were the best she had ever had in her life. She asked for second and third helpings. I never told her the ingredient that made them taste so good. She probably would never have enjoyed them or eaten them again. Secrets?

One of the things I enjoyed most about private practice in Chattanooga was the political atmosphere in the hospital. Not many people wanted to serve on the multiple committees and in leadership positions that took a lot of time and paid zero. At Erlanger Hospital I started out by being chairman of the emergency room committee. I was in that position when Erlanger became a level one trauma center and bought their first Bell & Howell helicopter for transporting patients to the emergency room. It cost over $900,000. It also required three pilots per day. This was one of the advancements in trauma medicine that was learned during the Vietnamese war. Many medical advances are made during wartime. The "golden hour" was established and proven. Many lives were saved by rapid transport within the first hour of injury to a level one trauma hospital.

I also enjoyed being on the credentials committee at another local hospital. A physician with whom I had graduated from medical school had applied for membership on the medical staff. When someone applied for privileges, they presented a list of references from previous hospitals where they had been on staff. It was my idea to call people listed on their list of references for extra information. This physician I knew showed up at the hospital in scrubs and a suit coat. I thought he was eccentric even in medical school. When I called the references about this physician, I was able talk with one of the doctors listed. After vowing me to secrecy, he told me that this physician had an office manager in his practice who disappeared with over $500,000 that was embezzled. The body of the manager was found with no head, no hands, and no feet. No one had ever proved that any of this was associated with the physician applying for a place on our medical staff. However, after a lengthy discussion with the credentials committee members, the physician decided to move to another area. Secrets!

After coming back to Chattanooga, there was another doctor in practice there who had been raised very similarly to me. His father had been a Church of God minister and he probably was the second physician to come out of the same background. He was in the doctor's lounge at Erlanger Hospital late one evening "making out" with a nurse on the couch. They were interrupted by housekeeping. The housekeeping staff did not report the event or make a fuss. But when she returned later and they were still in the act and questionably inebriated with drugs or alcohol, security was called. I heard there were later difficulties with legal problems associated with drugs and family relationships.

Not long after I got back to Chattanooga, Elvis Presley passed away. I heard all the stories about how he had not really died and it was all some sort of a conspiracy. Since I had first met Elvis outside his house in 1957 in Memphis, I had followed his career while I was in medical school and his relationship with Dr. Nick, George C. Nichopoulos, who was his personal physician. He had evidently written lots of prescriptions for Elvis and eventually lost his license to practice medicine. When Elvis passed away in 1977, one of my classmates was working in pathology at Baptist Hospital. He helped perform the autopsy on Elvis and said he was sure Elvis was really dead because he had held Elvis' heart in his hands.

Just west of Chattanooga is a town called Whitwell which was right in the middle of the Sequatchie Valley. I had an older man from the valley bring in his youngest daughter who was eighteen years old to have her tubes tied. She was very slow mentally. By history I found out that the father had two children by his first daughter and one child by his second daughter. He wanted his youngest daughter to have her tubes tied so he could continue "using her." I reported him to the state Family Services and they suggested that I tie the tubes of the young girl because there was nothing they could do legally to help. Family Services was quite familiar with the family and the situation. In order to prevent further inbreeding, I did a tubal ligation on the young girl. I suggested that the man have a vasectomy but he emphatically refused. Medicaid covered all expenses. Another governmental system gone wrong.

One doctor with whom I graduated from medical school had an eidetic memory. He used to make money during school by playing cards at a casino in Memphis. He knew the exact number of cards that had been played and his chances of drawing toward a full house or inside straight or flush. He came to Chattanooga as the chief of radiology at Erlanger. He had a lung resection due to cigarette smoking but persisted smoking cigars and inhaling deeply. We were shocked and very saddened when he went to his daughter's wedding in Mexico and due to a parasailing accident was killed in the prime of his life and after surviving cancer of the lung.

I continued my interest in baseball and the New York Yankees while I was in private practice. In 1978 the Red Sox had once led the American League East by ten games. The Milwaukee Brewers were in second place at the time and the New York Yankees were in third place. One of the urologists was very short in stature and an avid but obnoxious Boston Red Sox fan. He approached me one day in mid-July after the Yankees had fallen to fourteen games behind the Red Sox. He spouted, "I bet you $100 that the Yankees won't finish in first place this year." Laughing, I replied, "I don't have $100 to bet with you." He stomped off saying, "That doesn't make any difference!" The season ended with the Yankees and Red Sox tied for first place in the American League East. There was a one-game tiebreaker game played on 2 October 78. The Yankees won the game 5-4 and finished in first place ahead of the Red Sox. The next day the urologist walked up to me and without saying a single word, stuffed a $100 bill in my coat pocket. I said, "I told you I didn't have $100 to bet with you." "It doesn't matter, I made a bet," he muttered, turned, and stomped away. Little guy, big ego.

We occasionally got enough snow in Chattanooga to bring everything to a grinding halt. I remember on several occasions when the power was off or the phone just did not work correctly I would have a policeman come to the door of my house and knock to give me a ride to the hospital or let me use their phone to call the hospital or to just check on me.

I had a good friend who worked at Combustion Engineering and did office cleaning at the medical clinic we covered there. Her name was Sister Babe. She taught me about "tips" which was a local gambling system that blacks and others used on 9th Street in Chattanooga. The winning tip paid $1.20 for a 10-cent ticket or twelve times whatever you bet. It was based on the high scores from the previous day's baseball games, football games, or basketball games, and was a year-round system. It was honest and could not be fixed. Of course the guy who ran it, who was a local restaurateur, made 10 percent off the top. Police knew about it and even pulled "tips." Sister Babe also sold her food stamps at 50 cents on the dollar. I always wondered if it made a difference who you were or how you dressed in order to use food stamps. I bought $20 worth of food stamps from her. In my sports coat and tie, my usual attire for making rounds at the hospitals, I went into the Red Food Store. I bought groceries and paid with the food stamps and nobody ever asked a question. Using the credit card type food stamps today, no one has to be embarrassed giving paper food stamps to pay for groceries. I saw a lady offer to buy groceries with her food stamps for another woman if she would give her cash back for the food stamps she used.

I realized that the government had many people dependent on them when, in my training, I saw a fifteen-year-old child who had been raped give birth. The baby was there with her fifteen-year-old mother, her thirty-year-old grandmother, her forty-five-year-old great-grandmother, her sixty-year-old great-great-grandmother and her seventy-five-year-old great-great-great-grandmother. Six generations all present for the birth of a new baby who had been conceived violently. They were rewarded with a picture in the newspaper. Another example of government gone wrong.

By staying in the Army reserves, I had to spend two weeks every summer at "summer camp" at an Army post in the United States. In the midst of difficulties with number two, I went to a summer camp at Camp Shelby, Mississippi in 1984. It was during those two weeks of my absence that number two made plans for a divorce.

I used the two weeks at summer camp to take stock of myself and decided to stand up for myself and my family. Number two had other ideas. After her being in charge, there was no way she would allow me to become head of my family. She was in total control. On returning home, she refused to let me back in the house. I insisted that I needed some clothes and a place to stay until we could work things out. She allowed me to come into the house to pack a few things. I wanted to take my gold necklace and her written summary of abuse by her father. I tried to slide these in my pocket without notice but with the help of my oldest son, she grabbed the gold necklace, which she later sold, and tore up the summary of abuse by her father in front of us both. I spent the next few weeks living at my office which luckily had a shower. I could take the kids to my office overnight on weekends where they slept on air mattresses on the floor with me. That was the beginning of a very acrimonious divorce. When I had come back from summer camp she reminded me that she was the one who had taken my daughter from a private school and made her attend a public school "in order to save money" and that she had called my oldest son "a stupid sh.." on many occasions and there was nothing I could do about it. She failed to mention that several of my children had run away from home under her care and would do so again in the future.

From the very first of our marriage, she completely controlled everything we did. I accepted my part in the problems, but worked hard with my surgery to keep me from thinking about the situation and to continue providing financial support. When we went out to eat at a restaurant, she ordered food for everyone. She would wait for the order, bring it back to the table where everyone was seated waiting for her, and then give each person their food. Looking back, I should've tried harder to challenge these actions. She always controlled all of us. While we were shopping, we all had to walk around with our hands behind our backs or she would cause a loud and embarrassing scene. She said she thought we would break something we couldn't pay for. She had been able to convince all the children to agree with her, and they begin to contradict anything I said. I could not tell if they feared the situation but they were fearful of me.

Whenever number two did not take her medication, things were unbearable. If I could have forced her to take medication every day, maybe things could have worked out differently. She always said that medication made her feel "like a zombie." I had heard that same description from my cousin who was also bipolar. Medication made number two "normal" to us but took away the "highs," or manic pleasurable times for her. Without medication, the depressive cycles were unbearable. There were periods when I went without seeing my children and could not communicate with them at all.

I did not understand why she allowed me to visit with my fourth son but not with the other children. On one weekend visitation, I was able to lead Peter to salvation immediately after watching a Billy Graham movie about a father and his young son reestablishing a relationship after a divorce. We were sitting in my old gray GMC van. I was able to discern that Peter understood when he made a tearful decision to become a Christian. Then I understood that God allowed me to continue being with him for just this reason. Coincidence or miracle?

Events continued to disintegrate. My attorney asked me to make recordings of my visits with the older children. I actually carried a cassette tape recorder in my shirt pocket. Divorce proceedings were begun in 1983 and were quite voluminous, time-consuming, and expensive. We eventually had several court appearances and I was forced on several occasions to represent myself. There were multiple testimonies from number two, myself, and the kids in open court before a judge and other members of the audience. With a straight face, number two complained that I stuck needles in both her eyes on several occasions. She also stated that I placed firecrackers in her ear canals and exploded them. She never had any physical problems with her vision or hearing and could produce no records from doctors or witnesses of any problems with either. We all had to listen to her complaints. They were all lies! I have no idea how much of this presentation the judge believed, but for years it cost me my kids. I tried to bring up her summary of abuse by her father but she flatly denied that it ever happened. After the divorce was finished, I could no longer visit with my children except every two weeks. On many occasions number two would convince the older four not to go with me and only the youngest son Peter was ever allowed to visit with any regularity.

One occasion I was standing in front of the house when number two paraded all my children in front of me and had each one of them tell me they did not ever want to see me again. She then rounded them up and took them back inside the house. When I said I would like to talk to them again, she pulled a very large revolver and took a stance with her legs spread apart and both hands gripping the gun similar to a stance that the police would use. In fact, I later found out that she had a friend at the police department who had taught her this stance and assisted her in eventually setting me up. I reached forward thinking the revolver was a fake gun and that she was trying to scare me. On touching cold metal, I realized the gun was not plastic but real. I grabbed the barrel and twisted it down. She fired. A hole was blown in the front of the house which went through the wall into my oldest son's bedroom. I took the gun away, called the police, and gave them the gun. From a later credit card bill, I learned that I had not only paid for the gun but also for lessons to shoot it accurately. Even though I had paid for it, I never got the gun back but thank God, neither did she.

I met number three when I took the cassette tapes to be typed from the recordings that were made when I initially tried to pick up my children. Number three was a medical secretary at a local hospital and was very helpful to me in preparing the transcriptions for my encounters with number two and my children. She was the first person in my life I ever met who could respond openly, politely, and honestly about compliments. On one occasion I told her she was a very pretty lady and she actually said "Thank you." She didn't make an excuse as number one and number two always had about any compliment I gave them. They always replied that I was lying or wanted something.

The divorce from number two and the presence of my children with no regularity in my life led to many problems. After the bitter divorce from number two, I began dating number three. She was the most "normal" person I had ever met. It took a couple of months to get her to think of me as anything but a friend. Many times I had only my youngest son to visit and Peter and I spent good times with Cindy and her daughter. On one occasion we attended a circus performing at the Memorial Auditorium. We had seats near the front row of the mezzanine. It seemed we were very close to the trapeze artist who could hang by her teeth from the trapeze bar as it spun around. I remember my son watching her and saying, "Maw- Maw (my mother, his grandmother) could do that."

I was excluded from everyone but my immediate family. My work was all that kept me going. It was during this time in 1985 that I had a new patient come to my office. The sixty-year-old woman was obviously dying. She had had cancer of the cervix and the entire contents of her pelvis had been removed because of the cancer. She had metastatic disease to her bones and was having a lot of pain. I controlled her pain with narcotics. This was the usual accepted treatment for patients dying with cancer. Hospice does the same thing now. I will always believe that number two was aware of this patient and assisted police by telling them that I was selling prescriptions for pain medications to my patient. My attorney later told me that after I had treated this patient, the police had actually wired several patients to come to my office and try to get narcotics prescriptions for cash. All were unsuccessful. The tapes were never presented in court. I found that number two had actually dated one of the policemen heading the investigation.

Everything came as quite a surprise to me when I was arrested in my office. I had to wait over an hour in my office while they searched my patient files. The police were not answering any questions, not allowing me to call an attorney, and gave me no reasons for seizing patient records. Finally I was told that the charge against me was feloniously prescribing narcotics and conspiring to sell prescriptions.

When I was marched outside with my hands cuffed behind my back and placed into a police car, I understood. The television cameras were there. Number two knew ahead of time what was happening and had called the local stations. I was then taken to the police station, booked, and fingerprinted. Number three's car that I was driving that day was impounded.

I would've done much better to lie and say that I was using drugs and selling them to support a drug habit. I would have been sent to drug rehabilitation and things would've been much simpler. I could not lie. My truth in denying the charges caused me much expense, three days of trial, and a complete day of testifying. During the divorce, number two had demanded to be paid alimony and child support in cash. Even with my showing withdrawals from my account, she showed her cash deposits to the police and told him that I had paid her in cash just to support the charges.

After an all-day deliberation by the jury, I was convicted in June 1988 of feloniously prescribing narcotics to a dying cancer patient. The police had my patient testify on videotape because they were afraid she would die before the trial. She did. I thought it was obvious that she testified against me to get her drug charges dropped. She was selling half of her medication in order to have funds to live on and using the other half of her prescription for her pain. The police and attorneys never proved that I did anything but provide adequate care by giving pain medication to my cancer patient. The number of prescriptions I gave to the patient in my care (not counting the prescriptions she forged) was much less medication given by other physicians who treated similar cases. The number was miniscule compared to what is given today for similar patients.

The jury voted for the first time 10-1 against my conviction but one person held out. After a lengthy deliberation and pressure by the prosecutor to "wrap it up," everyone was happy to see a local doctor be convicted for anything connected with drugs. The charges for conspiracy were dropped.

Just before the trial, I believe number two asked the IRS for an audit of my taxes. A two-week intensive review of my tax returns showed nothing suspicious with my finances. I asked the agent if I could use this material in court to help prove my innocence but was told this was not possible. I was convicted and sentenced to three years in the Hamilton County Jail and fined $10,000. Two good friends lent me the money to pay the fine and it took me five years to repay them. I actually spent thirty days in the Hamilton County Jail early September 1988 to early October 1988.

While in jail I met the husband of the sister of a friend from my local church who became my protector. He was much larger than I and he had been in jail several times before. You can imagine what could've happened to a doctor and a naïve person like me in jail. Coincidence or miracle? I was allowed to work in the library and the prison chaplain was a member of our local church who also provided me with a month's worth of Bible study and met with me weekly. Coincidence or miracle? I had married number three in April 1985. She was with me through it all and went to the presiding judge and pled my case. My sentence was decreased to the one month spent and I was given an additional eight hundred hours of community service. I was allowed to return to my life outside jail. Coincidence or miracle?

From 1 December 1988 until just before Christmas, I was treated for codependency at Charter Lakeside Clinic in Memphis, Tennessee. The physician who represented me and helped me get my licenses back after the trial actually testified against me during the trial. He was not a surgeon and had never treated anyone who had been operated on for cervical cancer with a total pelvic exenteration (this is a major cancer operation where uterus, tubes, ovaries, and all lymph nodes in the pelvis are removed). He stated that I gave my patient too much pain medication.

Because of his conversations with number two before the trial, he had convicted me in his mind before he even met me. He actually apologized to me after the trial. Number two had told him I was violent and would physically hurt him. The first time I met him was after the trial. He asked me to meet in a public place and when we shook hands, he said, "Please, don't hit me." Dr. Dodd eventually became a friend and both he and the Tennessee Medical Foundation worked with me.

Charter Lakeside Clinic was where I learned about codependency. I was told I could not be a "knight in shining armor" or be "everything to all people" as I had told the admission committee in medical school I wanted to be. You can read many books about codependency as I did and come to your own conclusions. I came to mine. My treatment consisted of going out with my group to Toys "R" Us and buying a teddy bear that represented me. I carried a yellow and white teddy bear around with me all the time to discover my "inner child." I was told my problems stemmed from abandonment as a child and abuse by a cousin. I had to use a Bataka Encounter Bat to aggressively hit a bean bag which represented those who had damaged me—my father and cousin. If you didn't hit hard enough or long enough, you weren't doing the therapy correctly and were required to do it again. The games people make us play. If I had said I was addicted to narcotics, I would not have even been prosecuted but still would've had to go through the same treatment. The truth hurt and cost me much more than time and money. I had to be treated to return to "normal" again.

I was unemployed from January 1989 to May 1989. My eight hundred hours of community service were spent in Chattanooga working at a homeless shelter. I learned how to cook for fifty on a daily basis. We had breakfast and lunch for anyone who showed up and needed or asked for a meal. Moon Pies and Little Debbie's cakes were from local companies and were staples. On one occasion I had a large aluminum pot that I filled with pinto beans for the next day. As I was leaving for the day, I remembered that Mother had always added water for the beans to soak. I poured water in to fill the pot. The next morning there were beans everywhere. I had two pots full to cook for meals. "Slim" was in charge of the shelter and bought surplus products from a large food warehouse. He bought Campbell's soup for 10 cents a can. His grandson was collecting the soup labels for a school project and "Slim" took off all the labels from the cans for his grandson. I made some interesting soup with random fifty cans of soup I chose. Thank God there was a lot of tomato soup in the selection which made for a good base for what made up the rest of the soup. At least it was hot and nourishing. No one was turned away—lawyers, street people, winos, or doctors like me.

During and after finishing the eight hundred hours of community service, I looked for a job. It seemed everyone in Chattanooga was sympathetic but no one had a job for a disgraced surgeon. I got a call from the CEO of Fentress County General Hospital in Jamestown, Tennessee. He had grown up in Chattanooga and knew about the trial and results. He realized what had happened. He recruited me to fill a need he had in Fentress County for a general surgeon who was board certified who did not mind working in a rural area. I had and needed no further options. Coincidence or miracle?

Number three has always been supportive and had been there for me in everything that even remotely touched my life. I remember when we were walking out of the courtroom after my conviction, she stopped, held my hand, and told me she was with me through whatever happened. Cindy, my mother, and Aunt Odine were there with me the entire time and gave me total support. Thank God for righteous women. It has now been thirty years since that unbelievable time in my life. When I married number three, she had a five-year-old daughter who we combined with my five children. I adopted her child when she turned eighteen years of age. Times have not always been the best and I was not always the best father, but even the worst of times with number three and all the relationships in our families have never even come close to the pits of despair with number two. I guess in reviewing the situation you could say I was married to number one, divorced her, remarried her, and divorced her. Number one was two marriages. I married number two, divorced her, remarried her and divorced her. Number two was two marriages. However you look at it, number three or my fifth marriage, was the saving grace of my life. Cindy accepted me as I was with all my legal and personal problems. It was fascinating to notice that number two never spoke to any of the kids again after they rebuilt relationships with me. I can see by looking over all the problems that have occurred that God was in control of my life and through him I was directed and spiritually ordained to get where I am now. I have my father's Bible and even with the genealogy listed and updated, it is still a treasure.

My practice actually felt no effect from the "drug accusation" but my partners did not want to continue in a relationship. They had tolerated my marriage to number three, but they did not want to have any semblance of being associated with me after being convicted.

I married Cindy, number three, in Chattanooga, Tennessee, on April 12, 1985. We had a honeymoon in Bermuda. I promised her I would take her back on our twenty-fifth wedding anniversary and eventually made it there on our thirtieth anniversary. Now she wants to go back as often as possible. She deserves that after putting up with me for over thirty years. I believe she has an excellent start on sainthood also. Both her five-year-old daughter and my eight-year-old son participated in our wedding. Problems with number two never stopped.

She constantly drove wedges between me and my older children and then started to work on my eight-year-old son. Things were in constant turmoil. Cindy and I began our lives together attending the Church of God and finally found a home church. When we got married, the only things I asked of her were that she attend church with me and stop smoking. She immediately did both. I have failed both her and my youngest daughter in many ways but they have remained consistent and still love me.

After my horrid divorce from number two, the constant problems with my children, the conviction of feloniously prescribing pain medication, the time spent in jail, treatment for codependency, and then unemployment, there was nothing left for us in Chattanooga. Don

Downey had gotten in touch with me and offered an opportunity in Jamestown, Tennessee. We were ready to move. I had bought a large house on Missionary Ridge in Chattanooga where our family of three lived. It was much too large for the three of us. However, with all my real estate knowledge, I thought I knew what was best. It was called "Maison Blanc" because some of the marble in the front bathroom had come from the White House when Senator Kefauver was there and the White House was renovated. He had moved some of the marble to Tennessee and the owner of Chattanooga Bakery (Moon Pies) had built the house. I was "head over heels" in debt but found that was a usual place for me. We sold the house about three months after I had moved to Jamestown, Tennessee. Cindy remained until the house sold. An attorney's wife who had just been on a trip to Las Vegas and had won a million-dollar jackpot on the slot machines fell in love with the house and bought it from us with cash. I was able to break even and began life in Jamestown with nothing but my family. Coincidence or miracle?

CHAPTER 13

Jamestown was a town of sixteen hundred fifty people. We actually lived in Allardt, Tennessee, a town of 750 which was about five miles from the hospital. There was only a four-way stop in town. Fentress County was the poorest of the ninety-three counties in Tennessee. I was able to work there because my medical license was returned after codependency treatment and the other physicians in town would write prescriptions for narcotics for my surgical patients until I got my narcotic license back. I was truly accepted and appreciated by physicians and community. I remained in practice there for eighteen years. Coincidence or miracle?

The hospital in Jamestown, Tennessee, was a fifty bed facility. There were four other doctors practicing there when I arrived. An older physician who had been there "forever" did most of the general surgery until I arrived. I was the only board-certified surgeon who had ever been there. The hospital housed me in an apartment in one of the two local motels. It was approximately three months before Cindy was able to get everything moved to Jamestown. I was the only surgeon in Fentress County for the next eighteen years. I was always on call and when I went out of town on vacation or at a meeting, it was necessary to send surgical emergencies to another facility. There were two older partially trained family practice/surgeons who had been there for many years, a physician from India who did general practice, and an internist. The staff welcomed me and I felt at home for the first time in many years.

I remember the first day we were in Jamestown. I was taking call and dutifully had my beeper on my belt. The hospital administrator was showing us the county and helping us select a home. My beeper went off. There was a young lady in the Emergency Room who had an incompetent cervix and was miscarrying a six-month-old baby. The D.O. in the emergency room had pulled on the body of the baby which was protruding from the cervix of the patient. As the ER doc tugged, the body of the baby came out but the head of the baby was left inside the mother. I was called to take the patient to the OR to remove the head of the baby from the mother's uterus. It was necessary to remove the skull in a piecemeal fashion by crushing it. This was done to prevent an open surgery. She had had four pregnancies and had lost each at six months.

I found that I had to be very careful in what I said about anyone I met in Jamestown. Family relations were the same as many other previous small towns I had lived in. It seemed that everyone was either kin to or had been married to each other. When I was asked about my family, I jokingly told everyone that I had six children by six different wives. They believed me. In the first year or so that I was there a new young female employee came to work in dietary services. Her eyes were crossed and she had very poor oral care. I mentioned these facts one day during surgery and said that the new employee's family should've been taking care of her. The OR supervisor replied, "That's my sister and we are taking care of her." An older doctor in town had removed one ovary along with an ovarian cyst when she was in her early teens and then on another occasion in her teens removed the remaining ovary along with ovarian cysts. Therefore, she was sterile and a couple of years later I had to remove a very small juvenile uterus that was totally useless.

Jamestown, Tennessee, had a sister city in Muncie, Indiana. There even was a taxi service to take residents from Jamestown to Muncie. The major industry in Jamestown was the local shirt factory. I sewed up a laceration on a young boy in the ER. Being very busy and in a hurry, I closed the wound with a "running stitch." The mother looked at me and asked," Doc, do you know what kind of stitch that is?" I quickly answered, "Yes, that's a running lock stitch." "No, that's a hem stitch." Both of us were correct, but this confirmed the fact that many people who worked in Jamestown worked in the shirt factory. Jobs were few and far between.

Most young people who wanted to work went to Muncie, Indiana, for industrial jobs. The older family practitioner/surgeon had operated on a lot of people for appendicitis. He had a special way of marking the skin with the back of a scalpel before he made an incision. This supposedly made the incision and closure more anatomically correct; however, it marked the patient in a way anyone could identify anyone else who had had an appendectomy by the same surgeon. A young man had moved from Jamestown to Muncie looking for work and found a job at a factory there. When he arrived at work his first day it was very hot. On entering the factory, he removed his T-shirt. Across the factory someone yelled, "Hey, you're from Jamestown." The young man thought this was a good guess because he was new to the job. However, when the other man walked up to him, and looking at his abdomen, he said, "You also had your appendix removed by the surgeon in Jamestown." The young man was amazed and didn't understand how someone could have that information. Only when the second man pulled up his T-shirt and showed him an identical appendectomy scar did he understand that both of them had been operated on by the same person in Jamestown, Tennessee.

Jamestown and the entirety of Fentress County was a collection of "white people": there were no people of color. The local family practice doctor from India was married to a "white" nurse and had two sons, both of whom later became doctors. The boys were considered "half breeds" by the local high school students. There were two families where the father had been in the Army and brought home a Korean wife or as they were called in Jamestown, a "moose." Both mothers moved to Knoxville but left the kids in Jamestown with their fathers. In fact one of the sons became a nurse and worked with me in surgery. There were no black people in the community, or county; however, there were "poor whites." Some of the young women had left town and come back home with their "mixed" children. Some of the children had black fathers and two had Samoan fathers. The fathers didn't come back with the family.

The local McDonald's had a very difficult time finding people to work. I was told that a worker would have to have an income of approximately $21,000 to meet the free handouts from the government. In fact the McDonald's was closed for several months before someone finally bought the franchise and reopened the store. The owner survived by using teenagers to work. They used it as their beginning place in the work force. Most of the young women in the county who were not married and had children did not work. The government paid $200 a month per child for the support of the "fatherless" family. Interestingly, we were only fifteen miles from the Kentucky border. I had a patient who had four children. She received Medicaid benefits from the state of Tennessee and from the state of Kentucky. I promptly reported her. The response I got from the government Medicaid worker was "What do you want me to do? We have larger problems than that to deal with." Father government won again.

It was necessary for me to work in the emergency room when I started in Jamestown. Two of the local doctors had not gone on vacation for several years and immediately went on vacation. I think I lived in the emergency room for my first three weeks and saw most of their patients. Since their offices were closed, everyone came to the emergency room for care. It was called a "baptism by fire." Several patients used the emergency room for their entire care rather than go to a local doctor's office. The same is true today! One elderly lady had seventeen dogs and came to the emergency room with a chief complaint of "phlebitis." She really meant that the multiplicity of fleas in her house caused bites on her legs and thus the term, "flea-bitis."

I had my first introduction to a "savant" while in Jamestown. Ricky was an orderly in the hospital who came to the emergency room frequently to see if he could help. On one occasion we were very busy. A middle-aged woman had come in with an overdose of medication. Ricky asked if he could help. I gave the patient a dose of ipecac to induce vomiting, and I asked Ricky to assist by giving her twenty eight-ounce cups of water to drink. He religiously gave each cup until on the nineteenth cup she promptly vomited up all her medication and her upper set of false teeth. Of course the vomitus covered Ricky head to foot. You could hear him walk and "squish" for the next 30 minutes or so because his shoes were full of water. The patient complained bitterly about losing her false teeth. Later, Ricky sheepishly walked up and said, "I found her teeth." They were in the pocket of his white lab coat.

Ricky and his wife had two healthy normal boys. Their two daughters had been born with congenital brain, heart, lung, kidney, and intestinal deformities. Both girls passed away before six months of age. Ricky's personality was very flat and he always appeared serious. He and his wife seemed to always have problems. Once she was clinging to his pickup truck door outside of the emergency room trying to talk to him. "Let loose of my door. I'm leaving," he drawled. She hung on for dear life. Ricky drove her around the parking lot before she finally managed to drop to the ground with only abrasions.

Ricky could do magic with small engines. He had a job with John Deere and repaired the motors in lawn mower tractors. The company first became interested when they found he could reverse the gears in a John Deere lawnmower and make them go extremely fast. He actually had lawnmower "races" while in high school. John Deere gave him $30,000 worth of equipment. I heard he later sold the tools for $600. On one occasion, the company called Ricky and asked if he could help with a problem the company had with a small tractor engine. Ricky said, "Sure, hold the phone next to the engine and try to start it." The experts said, "You're gonna need to come here and look at the engine." Ricky adamantly responded, "Hold the phone next to the engine!" They did and tried to start the engine. Immediately he gave them the answer to their complex problem and the engine then started.

I worked in the emergency room on my first Christmas Eve there. I had a very memorable experience. My shift started as usual in the part of the hospital that never sleeps. It was busy, but no real emergencies. Some people had nothing better to do than spend an inordinate part of their evening in the waiting room at the ER to see a doctor who was unknown to them. I usually ordered enough blood work and X-rays to prevent a possible malpractice case or discover some unusual illness. Several weeks prior, I had picked Christmas Eve to work. I figured it would either be busy and the time would fly by quickly or it would be deathly quiet. Everyone knew that the mention of being "quiet" caused the worst of busy times to begin in the emergency room.

After three hours of mundane diagnoses and being as nice as I could, an eerie feeling of quietness started. Since I had lived in rural areas for most of my life, I knew that listening to the police scanner had replaced baseball as the national pastime and the people in Jamestown had carried it to an even higher level of importance. There were more scanners than cars in Fentress County and the one in the emergency room was on constantly. It supplied background music to the usual cacophony of medical sounds. "This is the sheriff and I'm on my way to the emergency room," erupted over the scanner. The local sheriff, in my opinion, was a capable law enforcement officer notwithstanding the fact that he had a speech impediment. I remember the story I first heard about the sheriff.

One of the nurses at the hospital had worked in the emergency room for many years. She was speeding through town coming to the hospital for her shift. The sheriff had pulled her over. When she rolled down her window, he asked, "Wet me see youh wicense." She replied, "Okay," and retrieved her driver's license from her purse and handed it to the sheriff. He quickly looked at both sides and grinned as if he had caught a serial killer. "It says heah that youh supposed to weah gwasses." He smirked knowing that he had at least caught her in an embarrassing situation. Quickly the nurse replied, "But I have contacts." This sheriff immediately replied, "I don't cauh who you know."

That night when the sheriff burst into the emergency room, he was puffing due to his extra weight. He was dressed in khaki pants and would have looked like one of the maintenance men except for the fact he had a large silver badge shaped like a star pinned to his shirt pocket. After slamming the door, he said "Hey, Doc, come with me." Since it was quiet and I had nothing going on in the emergency room, I couldn't resist an order from the local chief law enforcement officer. I put on my white coat so I could be recognized, but mostly because it was 36° outside and it was sleeting. As I went through the double doors in the back of the emergency room, I noticed that the police car was still running.

"Where's the fire, sheriff?" I said. He didn't reply until we were both in the front seat of the squad car.

"There's something I want you to see." He took off like a scalded dog which was the only speed the sheriff knew. We took a left on Highway 52 E. in front of the hospital and headed toward town. I was thankful not many people were out at 10:00 PM because of the road being slick and icy. We fishtailed onto the highway. Two blocks later we came to Main Street and turned right at one of the two traffic lights in town. Both lights were red. We went through them anyway. The sheriff had his red and blue lights on and his sirens blaring. "We're going to Shack Town." I had never been there but I knew it was only a few blocks away.

On the left when we got there and the car lights swept into the darkness, I noticed a bedraggled young woman with two small children. She was dressed in a very simple "house dress." It appeared to be a one-piece cotton dress that had been worn and faded so much that the yellow and blue floral pattern could hardly be recognized. She wasn't protected from the elements at all. A small boy of about four was on her right, clutching her leg, and an eight-year-old girl was standing along her left side. All were shivering from the cold wetness of the sleet. In the poor light, it was still excruciatingly obvious that the mother had multiple bruises covering most of her arms and face.

The sheriff jumped out of the car and asked, "What's happening?"

All the woman could say was, "Inside." That's a memory still etched in my brain of the three people standing in front of a small white-framed house. The mother and daughter had tears discernible from the wetness on their faces from the cold rain and sleet. The little boy did nothing but stare straight ahead. There were no further words from any of them. I quickly followed the sheriff up on the front porch and through the door that was left open. He had been prepared for what we saw by the call that had come from the dispatcher earlier. I was not. The small living room was well lighted. On the right hand was a Christmas tree that was decorated by a caring mother with help evidently from her two kids. There were homemade paper ornaments, carefully cut out and colored with crayons. There were flashing lights of red and green. Icicles were carefully placed and some were thrown by the handfuls, hanging precariously from the lower branches. A silent angel was on top overlooking the entire scene. Underneath the tree were a few gifts wrapped with white paper and red and green bows. Next to the presents was a body, limbs askew, with his throat cut from ear to ear. Only then could I see the extraordinary amount of blood everywhere including the presents and tree apron.

"O, my God!" was the only thing the sheriff uttered. I mentally agreed with him. Evidently in a drunken stupor after work, the father had come home and verbally and physically abused the ones closest to him. Then in a moment of depression and guilt, had gone to the kitchen next to the living room and taken a butcher knife and used it on himself. You could actually see the "hesitation" marks on the skin of his neck before he finally cut deep enough to completely disgorge himself of blood in the eight or ten steps from the kitchen sink until he fell in front of the Christmas tree with the knife still clinched in his fist.

The sheriff drove me back to the emergency room. Less than an hour had expired since we had left. The silence was deafening. The rest of the Christmas Eve in the emergency room passed uneventfully.

Over ten years later, a newly hired eighteen-year-old admission clerk came up to me and said, "Hi, Dr. Carroll, I bet you don't remember me." Before I could respond, she told me her name. The mental picture of her standing next to her mother and brother returned to me in a flash.

For several moments I was lost, but my thoughts returned to the admission clerk who was standing in front of me. "Yes, Jennifer, I remember who you are," I exclaimed. She turned and went back to the front admission office.

Jamestown had a mayor who tried to think of ways to expand industry. He started a yard sale on Highway 127 that ran through the center of the town. The Highway 127 Yard Sale eventually ran from Addison, Michigan, down through Jamestown to Gadsden, Alabama. However, "America's biggest and longest yard sale" all started in Jamestown. Local entrepreneurs lined both sides of the road to sell goods, food, and antiques. Congestion caused a lot of accidents which I guess you could say helped the hospital business.

Laparoscopic surgery was a new technique in the mid-1980s. In my residency, I had learned to remove gallbladders by making an incision under the right ribs, through the skin, muscles, and fatty tissue, to get to where the gallbladder sits just underneath the liver. This was called an "open" technique and required the patient being in the hospital for approximately five days. Laparoscopy was very different and a new procedure that few surgeons understood but all wanted to learn.

Most of the people in private practice did not have time to attain formal training from a university residency. In fact most of the impetus for laparoscopic surgery was driven from the private practice of medicine. The universities were very slow to pick up the procedure. I wanted to do these laparoscopic surgical procedures so it was necessary for me to learn in some way.

One of the earliest and best courses was offered in Nashville. Before attending, I had several patients who had heard of the procedure come to me asking to be the first of my patients to have the new procedure carried out. Dr. Eddie Joe Reddick was the person who taught me how to do the surgery. He made a lot of money just teaching the new technique. I heard he eventually went into country music to try his luck but after losing a lot of money, he went back to teaching surgeons how to do laparoscopic cholecystectomies. When I was in Nashville for the training, there were several other surgeons from all over the country attempting to learn the new technique. They were all worried. How could they explain to any patient that they had never done this procedure laparoscopically and have anyone allow them to perform the surgery for the first time. I laughed and told them that in the rural area where I practiced, I already had a list of patients who wanted to be my first guinea pig. After first hearing didactic lectures from Dr. Reddick, it was necessary to scrub with him in surgery on two cases. The total cost for the one-day didactic lecture was only $2000. For an additional $1500, I could scrub with him on two surgeries. He treated me like a resident and was constantly critical of my help. I mentioned the amount of money his time was costing me and I told him I didn't intend to be treated that way. I had come there to learn and didn't enjoy being treated like a resident. He laughed and was much nicer to me after that.

In order to begin doing the new procedure, I needed to obtain the necessary equipment that included scopes, cameras, ports, new long instruments, and television-like screens. I could not convince the hospital administrator that this was going be a procedure that would become commonplace. It was necessary for me to go to the bank and borrow $50,000 and then find a company that had the equipment. After we accumulated the necessary instrumentation, the first gallbladder that I performed took three hours and forty-five minutes. The team in the OR cheered. I'm not sure if it was for finally finishing the procedure or that it was the first one done in that small rural community. The procedure, which took at least an hour to do "open," now has become a routine surgery that takes approximately thirty minutes to perform on an outpatient basis. No longer is it necessary to keep the patient in the hospital for five days. I kept extensive records on the first one hundred patients on whom I did a laparoscopic cholecystectomy. My mother was number ten on my list. She refused to have anyone else do her surgery.

The procedure was very successful and was frequently performed. It was done outpatient with the patient going home the same day only a few hours after surgery. It took over two years but the hospital paid me back, although without interest.

Several years later one of the physicians in town decided to do gallbladder surgery after attending the same course I had in Nashville. When he came back I assisted him in doing fifteen to twenty cases. Everything went well with those but when he started doing them on his own, two of his first four patients had severe complications leading to lawsuits. Being chief of surgery again required me to have to limit what some surgical practitioners could do.

Several other physicians in the area began doing laparoscopic gallbladder surgery. Approximately thirty miles from where I was located, I had one surgeon who was trained in his residency to do only laparoscopic surgery. When he found he could not remove a gallbladder laparoscopically, he did not know how to convert to an "open" case. I received a call and hurriedly drove to the other hospital to assist him in doing an "open" surgery. Years later a physician who had been trained to do bariatric surgery came to our small facility to start a hospital-based practice. He could not do an "open" hernia because he had never seen one done in his training; he had only repaired hernias laparoscopically.

I'll never forget the first time as a practicing physician in this rural area that I had a scared-looking patient come in the emergency room. The young man stood up straight as an arrow just inside the emergency room door. While observing the patient from the nurse's station, I wondered what story would come from this person. An accompanying friend ran around to where I was sitting and blurted out, "Hey, Doc. You gotta help him. He has a vibrator up his butt." After X-raying the patient, I found that it would require going to surgery and using spinal anesthesia to remove the vibrator. After a lengthy time of attempting to remove the large plastic object from his rectum, I looked at the x-ray again. I confirmed the written report that a 6-inch long vibrator was in his rectum. With adequate retraction I finally grasped the end of the long green vibrator and pulled it out. I asked the patient offhandedly, "Do you want this back?" Since he was under spinal anesthesia it was quite easy for him to respond, "Yeah, Doc. That's my mother's vibrator." The nurse working with me would not clean the vibrator off but slammed it in a plastic garbage bag, handed it to the patient, and angrily responded, "Then you can clean it off yourself!"

The next two instances of foreign bodies in rectums came from the same person: a morbidly obese prison guard at a youth facility. He came to the emergency room with a story that he had been taking a shower, slipped, and fell on an object in the shower. He admitted that the object had inadvertently entered his rectum and was inside him. I could not tell on X-ray what the object was. He was taken to surgery, and I found a spritz bottle inside his rectum. This was quite an experience for the surgical team to find not only was there a plastic bottle with the spray attachment present but also that there was still fluid inside the bottle. This patient did not want to take the bottle back with him. He came back about three months later with a similar story of taking a shower and falling on the couch where there were objects that were forced up his rectum. At surgery he had a shot glass and an 8-inch cucumber removed. When he awakened from surgery, I told him I was going to report these incidents to his employer. I worried because he worked in a youth detention center. I felt these were inappropriate and questionable actions for anyone especially those who worked with kids. He never showed up again. I did report him to his superiors but never found out if he was reprimanded.

One evening in the emergency room an eighty-year-old lady who had had a previous right hip replacement came in. She had a posterior dislocation of her prosthesis and was in a lot of pain. It was a trying experience to attempt to put a hip back in place after a surgical repair had been performed. We gave medication for relaxation to this elderly lady and had her lying on an emergency room stretcher. In order to reduce the dislocation, I had a male nurse who was young and much stronger than I stand up on the stretcher and pull her leg straight up while I pushed down on her pelvis.

The little old lady looked up at the young male nurse and said, "Have you ever thought about having sex in this position?" The nurse got down from the stretcher and refused to help me any longer. We had to transfer the patient to Cookeville for relocation of her hip by an Orthopedist.

In a small rural area, it was necessary to do many esophagogastroduodenoscopies and colonoscopies. I remember an elderly lady who needed to have a colonoscopy due to her rectal bleeding. I had talked to her husband Charles about her needing the procedure. He was agreeable. As we were putting her to sleep and I started the procedure using the usual colonoscope, she said, "O, Charles, you know I never liked it that way." Amazing the secrets you can learn under anesthesia.

I had a young lady with four children come in my office asking for a tubal ligation. We had a long conversation and agreed that four children was a nice family. We'd filled out the necessary paperwork to begin the approval for her surgery. When we got things set up, she asked that I perform a vasectomy on her husband at the same time. Again, we had a long conversation. I told her that it was not necessary for both her and her husband to be sterilized for there to be no more children. She agreed with me, but very adamantly said, "No, Doc, you don't understand. My husband is going to always be responsible for these children and will never leave me and have another family on his own!" The next Friday, I did a tubal ligation on my patient and a vasectomy on her husband. Smart lady in a rural setting.

As in most parts of the country, we had a drug problem in our small town. I was called one evening for possible surgery. On arriving at the emergency room, I met a young man who had worked as a technician in our laboratory. His small intestines were hanging out of the upper part of the right side of his abdomen. I had no choice but to take him immediately to surgery. We were able to remove his gallbladder cut half into by the knife used during the fight that broke out after a busted drug deal. The knife not only cut his gallbladder in half but had cut his duodenum, or the first portion of his intestines just beyond his stomach, in half. After removing the gallbladder, I sewed up his duodenum and placed a stent through it by using a nasogastric tube through his nose into his stomach and around past where the duodenum had been repaired. I thought he was one lucky man to have gotten this far. In the lower part of his abdomen, I noticed a large collection of blood in his pelvis. On further examination I found that the vena cava coming up from his pelvis had been cut. It was necessary to call an emergency room nurse to immediately come to the OR to help give adequate retraction to expose the injured area. I was able to see that the vena cava had a large laceration across it just below the kidneys. There was a lot of bleeding but we were able to control it. I then asked for special sutures to repair the vena cava. Of course there were no such sutures to be found in our emergency room or surgery or anywhere else in the hospital. Being used to "flying by the seat of my pants," I then used a small Prolene or monofilament suture like fishing line to repair the vena cava. I did a lot of praying during the case as I do in all my surgical cases. Postoperatively the patient had no problems whatsoever. He was in the hospital for approximately one week and went home. I saw him back in my office a week later and, of course, he had no insurance and or funds to pay his bill. He was very thankful and told me so. Miracle or coincidence?

I have a painting in the hall outside my office of a surgeon standing at the operating table with Jesus standing behind him with His hand on the surgeon's shoulder. Many times in my early surgical career I did things that I thought were "impossible" during procedures. After these procedures, I would pat myself on the back and say, " What a great surgeon you are." Only later in my life did I realize that it was not me but Christ who worked through me.

I was so content in my situation in this rural area that my weight ballooned up to 385 pounds. Frequently I was able to play Santa Claus and did not require any extra padding. Dressed as Santa I would ride on the fire engine at the end of the Rotary Christmas parade. The parade was about a mile and a half long and after riding for about an hour, I went past the hospital and ended in front of the local nursing home. The certified registered nurse anesthetist who put patients to sleep for me had a son who was five years old. His wife was a pharmacist and was standing with the little boy, who is now physician, as I climbed off the back of the fire truck in my Santa Claus outfit. I turned around and saw the pharmacist with her son. "Hello, Gabe," I said. His eyes were as big as saucers as he looked at his mother and exclaimed, "Mamma, Santa Claus knows my name!" As I was walking back over to the shirt factory where I had parked my car, another little boy, the son of a nurse in the ER, said, "Mamma, why is Santa Claus walking?" "He's going over to find where he left Rudolph and his sleigh parked by the shirt factory," his mother quickly responded.

A forty-four year old lady was sent to me after her family practice doctor had found she had symptomatic gallstones. She had also been seen by her internal medicine doctor and cleared for surgery. She had an eighteen-year-old daughter who was an only child and "fixing to" get married. I did my usual physical exam but, after being cleared by two other doctors, it was limited to the upper part of her abdomen where her gallbladder and stones were. When the CRNA who gave anesthesia for me had the patient lying on the surgical table already asleep, I noticed that she had a mass in her lower abdomen. I said, "Either she has a large ovarian tumor or she is pregnant." It was not yet mandatory to obtain a pregnancy test before surgery on a woman during her childbearing years. However it became protocol after her pregnancy test came back positive. We found out that the patient was in the second trimester of her pregnancy and about four months along. I explained the situation to her husband who was waiting outside surgery. He was surprised but asked that we go ahead and take her gallbladder out. I went back in and removed her gallbladder without any difficulty. I was able to follow her throughout the rest of her pregnancy and she did well. It is now known that surgery during the second trimester usually causes no problem either for the mother or the baby. When she awakened, I told her that her gallbladder and stones were out but she was pregnant. Her husband was with her and both were very happy that she was pregnant and that her gallbladder had been removed. Her eighteen-year-old daughter got married and had a baby girl just a few months after her younger sister was born. Right before I left to come to Florida, I was able to see the father and his ten-year-old beautiful blonde-headed happy little girl at the county fair.

Jamestown Regional Medical Center was located in Jamestown and was in the middle of very beautiful country on top of the Cumberland Plateau. According to many people, there was a "pristine beauty" to the area. There was a plan at one time to have a railroad run from Nashville through Jamestown to Portsmouth, Virginia, which is one of the largest ports for export in the continental United States. After several years of trying, it was decided to not change any of the "pristine beauty" of the area. No one ever wanted to talk about the fact most of the young people who finished high school and preferred to work in their home county had to leave and go to other larger towns for jobs. I still think a large part of the problem existed because of the "environmentalists" who were against any change. I watched the same mentality affect Clewiston, Florida, the small town where I am now practicing. The "environmentalists" in Florida would rather have the Everglades than the people who live here. Most of the people who live on the coast have blamed agriculture and the people who work in the sugar industry for any problems that occur on the "beaches." They actually say that if Lake Okeechobee should flood and the people not return to the area, then all the problems with be solved. Environment over people?

We had started a family Amway business in Chattanooga and continued while in Fentress County and still maintain the business today. Another "secret." Most of our business was done and still is done out of town. We were at an Amway meeting on a Sunday morning when a minister who pastored a megachurch asked the audience of about two thousand if there was a "Leonard Carroll" present. I was both shocked and amazed. I stood and acknowledged that I was there. He told the story of how my dad had, on many Sundays, picked up him, his mother, and his four brothers and sisters and had taken them to church. This had happened when Dad pastored the small Church of God in Anderson, South Carolina. This minister said his father was an alcoholic. Because my father had been kind to his family and taken them to church, his entire family had been led to the Lord. From this early encounter, he became a minister. He now pastored a church of ten thousand people and had reached hundreds of thousands of people with the gospel of Jesus Christ. I never realized that my father had done this. That minister on that Sunday gave me a new perspective of my father. It was difficult for me, but I asked forgiveness from my father even though he had passed away years before. Coincidence or miracle?

Another reason I remained busy in Jamestown was that I had to work the emergency several nights and weekends per month in order to keep my income where I wanted it. I was in private practice and the hospital did not contribute to my income. I was working one night in the emergency room when a prisoner was brought in. He had cut himself purposefully on the arm with a razor blade just to get out of the jail, break the monotony, but most of all to get pain medication. It was necessary for me to suture the cut to his arm so I used xylocaine as a local anesthetic. On injecting the laceration, he yelled, screamed, and jumped. I actually drove an inch-and-a-half long needle through his skin into the left forefinger of my gloved hand. Being in surgery, I had had many instances where I had operated on patients with AIDS and hepatitis C. It was common for me and my patient to have blood drawn immediately and again in three months after a needle stick to make sure that I had not contracted either of these dread diseases. However, when the prisoner jerked his arm and I stuck a needle in my finger, more blood tests were required from both of us. His blood was positive for both. Imagine my surprise when four weeks later I was told that I was positive for hepatitis C. Poetry has always been a part of my life and I wrote this:

Hepatitis C

Even working a busy surgical practice
Permits working the emergency room.
In a small town
Eight to ten shifts a month

I've seen it all.
Two or three times.
A vibrator lost in a dark, moist recess.
A shot glass and a cucumber.
Even a half-full spritz bottle.
Medical problems.
Surgical are always the best.
Orange jumpsuit comes in
From the county jail.
When there's nothing to do
Cutting your arm with a razor
Is better than cramped quarters.
He is well known.
Positive for hepatitis C and AIDS.
Twenty-five gauge needle goes in.
Xylocaine with epinephrine stings.
May be a little show on his part.
With a yell and jump
An inch-and-a-half blue-hubbed needle
Has my left forefinger skewered.
They draw both our blood.
I already know what his results are.
I forget.
Amy, the infection control nurse calls
One month later.
Have you seen the results?
They're in the office.
Drugs for treatment.
Varied side effects.
No one wants to treat
A sixty-four-year-old surgeon/ER doc.
Thank God I only have
Hepatitis C.

Thank God ten years later now as we live in Florida, I no longer test positive for Hepatitis C. Miracle or coincidence?

On 9 September 2001, I went to New York City for a general surgery review course in preparation for the recertification exam for the American Board of Surgery. I stayed at the Southgate Tower Suite Hotel at 371 7th Avenue at the corner of 31st and 7th Avenue. I got to bed early that Sunday night. Monday morning 10 September, we had lectures from 0800 that morning until 1900 that night. The schedule was the same for Tuesday 11 September. I had left my phone charging in my hotel room. I walked down and had a continental breakfast and was seated in class for the beginning of the first lecture. A neurosurgeon was first to lecture and shortly after he began, I heard lots of noise from outside. I was sitting in the back of the room next to the projectionist who had earphones on evidently listening to news. The first thing I heard was "O, Sh..!" I later read a study that showed that "O, Sh.." is the most common utterance by the pilot before a plane crashes. Many times just hearing these two words caused the second pilot, who was usually faced away from the pilot, to eject just before crash landing. The projectionist then sprinted to the front of the room and whispered in the instructor's ear.

"We're under attack from terrorists," were the next words heard from the lecturer. Then, "I'm going home to be with my family." The loud noises from outside turned out to be fire engines and police cars with sirens blasting as they went past. As the instructor ran from the room, everyone was in disarray. I immediately left the lecture hall and went back to my room to get my phone. There were two messages. One from my wife telling me she loved me and to please be careful. She knew I was in New York but had no idea where I was in relation to the Twin Towers. She told me later she had called the hotel and they really didn't know what was going on. My oldest son left a message, "I should've known you would be in the middle of everything." My cell phone stayed on for the next two days and was one of few phones that actually worked during the whole situation as it developed.

While I was in my room getting my cell phone, I had thoughts of sitting down, watching television, and not leaving the room. I was really scared but I hurried downstairs. I found that a bus had already picked up several of the surgeons and taken them to somewhere north of our location. A second bus came and took us two blocks from Ground Zero. With the help of local police, we broke into a pediatrician's office. We took supplies, masks, IV fluids, and came back out on the street. There were approximately 3 inches of grayish dust and debris on the sidewalks, and there was paper and confetti-type material floating down through the air. We put masks on in order to breathe. One of the street vendors passed out juice to drink because of the intense heat. We were on our way toward Ground Zero when policemen came running up the street toward us and said, "The first building is down and the second building is going to fall." I had no idea what he was talking about. He told us that we had to make our way to Chelsea Piers. I didn't know where that was or how to get there. One young man standing beside his car on the street said, "I know where it is, get in my car." Ten of us packed in his car and he drove a couple of blocks to Chelsea Piers. A large movie studio was there that was used for a Michael J Fox television production. An ice rink on the second floor was used as a temporary morgue. We found that in New York the EMTs were in charge of the disaster program. As physicians, we were to back them up.

We set up a fifty-station makeshift hospital. There were very few people who actually came in with injuries. In fact the fifty stations were closed down to two stations for the evening and night. I was one of the two physicians to stay up all night waiting for any patients to show up. It was about 0200 on 12 September before I knew what had happened. Someone found a television and we watched the news as the two airplanes flew into the Twin Towers. Time drug by.

We treated very few people. Later that morning we were escorted back to the hotel. My primary purpose for being in New York was to attend the review course for general surgery. That was a poor second after what happened. We had several more review lectures for the next three days. My first concern was my family in Tennessee who were within an hour and a half of Oak Ridge where much of the nuclear research was carried out. I really wanted to go home but there was no way to get out of New York City. All rental cars were taken and no planes were flying. On 15 September, at 0700 Saturday morning I was able to catch a Greyhound bus and head home. It was a local bus and we stopped many times along the way picking up packages which were placed in the luggage compartment under the bus. We came through Washington DC and were able to see the damage done at the Pentagon. Coming through Tennessee, the closest place to Jamestown was Crossville about thirty-five miles away. The driver told me they were not stopping there. I was finally able to convince him to take a smoke break at a Huddle House close to Interstate 24 near Crossville. Cindy met me there at 0200 in the morning. I still to this day don't understand why I was there in New York City. Coincidence or miracle?

The state of Tennessee incorrectly thought that they could solve the Medicaid problem by developing their own state insurance program. TennCare was established. The state government had many insurance companies approach them. Most of the companies took a ten to fifteen percent management fee, went bankrupt over the next several months, and then walked away with a lot of money just as Medicare had manipulated reimbursement in the 80s when I worked in Chattanooga. The US government had forced me to accept Medicare that paid approximately thirty percent of the amount paid by the insurance companies. Then the insurance companies decreased their reimbursement to exactly the same amount Medicare paid. TennCare eventually took about sixty-five percent of the state budget. The privately-held insurance companies like Blue Cross found that the state would have to accept all the high-risk patients they had been insuring. Patients with AIDS; chronically ill patients; patients with preexisting conditions; liver, kidney, and heart transplant patients eventually ended up on the doorstep of the state of Tennessee. Many people who had no insurance moved to the state. I signed many contracts to provide care for TennCare patients and I provided the care. When I left in 2007, the insurance companies owed me over $200,000. I had a choice given me to settle for one cent on the dollar for a total reimbursement of $2000 for the work I had done or I could accept nothing at all. That's one of the main reasons we moved—along with no longer having ice, sleet, snow, a surgical practice under TennCare, and having to work ten 12-hour shifts in the ER each month. All these were affecting my health. Cindy finally said, "We need to move to Florida!"

Using all of my real estate skills, we began looking at the coasts of Florida. I purchased several lots on the ocean as a possible future or second home. I was able to resell these lots because it seemed someone always wanted the lots more than I did. In addition to the coast, we had looked in the northern part of the state but in order to find a place that stayed warm all the time, we considered South Florida. When we started looking in earnest, I decided that I would not be happy in any place unless it was rural. I remembered "if you cut the coast off of Florida, the rest of the state is country." I received a call from a "headhunter" who was looking for a board-certified surgeon and asked, "Have you ever thought about moving to Florida?" I stuttered, "I'm not looking for anywhere in Florida unless it's rural and in South Florida." He replied, "Do you know where Clewiston is?" On googling the area, I found that all our requirements were met. We found the town of seventy-five hundred on the Southwest corner of Lake Okeechobee. In the winter, the temperatures occasionally drop into the 40s and on two occasions in the last eleven years have reached thirty-one degrees.

Cindy decided the best way to leave Jamestown was to sell everything we could possibly do without and begin anew in Clewiston. We had a local auction company come to our house. We sold everything we could, from lawnmowers, clothes, beds, television sets, to personal items. Amazing how much a family can accumulate in eighteen years of living.

It was necessary for me to get my Florida medical license. Florida does not reciprocate with any other state licensing board. To do this, I had to take a "general medicine examination." Thanks to the emergency room work I had done in Jamestown, the exam was not difficult. Coincidence or miracle?

I believe the medical hierarchy in Florida believed that most people including physicians came to Florida to retire. "Retirement" is another word not found in the Hebrew language. I had no intentions of retiring and worked hard to convince people of that. Due to my previous problems with my license and conviction, it was necessary to have a meeting with the Florida State Board of Medical Examiners. I had interviewed with Dr. Forbes at Hendry Regional Medical Center, and with his support and the support of the hospital administrator, it was possible for us to move to Clewiston in January 2007.

CHAPTER 14

Cindy always had the ability to pick the correct house for our family. We found a home approximately 1-1/2 miles from the hospital, a California-style house. Since we had auctioned off most of our possessions before we moved, she slept on a mattress in our new bedroom and for comfort I slept in a reclining chair for the first year we lived in Clewiston while she decided what she wanted and how to decorate.

I began work on 1 February 07. Instead of being in private practice, I was now a hospital employee. A different way of thinking was required. I was no longer the boss but had a boss, or practice manager. Most physicians have a tendency to decrease the amount of work when they become an employee. However, since there had been no surgeon in the area for several months, a lot of Medicare and Medicaid surgical cases had backlogged. I did over eight hundred surgical cases during the first year I was here. Dr. Forbes was a real mentor for me. He told me many stories about his practice and working in Florida and helped me realize that if you operated and everything went well, a patient told another three people. If the surgery didn't go so well, the patient usually told twenty-seven other people. Look it up, there is a study that confirms these numbers.

Here I am at a "Critical Access" twenty-five-bed hospital in another rural area and another small town. I have enjoyed doing general surgery and feel that I am one of a dying breed of physicians. My surgeries have included trauma with chest tubes, laparoscopic surgeries, tonsillectomies, circumcisions, cancer of the penis in an AIDS patient, hysterectomies in AIDS patients, endoscopies, and innumerable other surgeries. Nowadays, things have become too specialized, in my opinion, but problems are all the same anywhere.

The area is populated with about twenty-five percent whites, about twenty-five percent blacks, and over fifty percent Hispanics. Many of the Hispanics are illegal and speak no English. Tammy is black and my CMA. Alex is Hispanic and my interpreter and patient coordinator. My practice manager is from Boston, Massachusetts. The nurses are different in name but not demeanor. They can be matched with nurses from my training, at a fifty-bed hospital in the Army, and a seven hundred fifty-bed hospital in Chattanooga. Most of the doctors are the same.

I never realized I had an accent but I guess living in Tennessee for over fifty years makes me eligible for one. I have had several PA students think I'm saying "special" when I describe the "spatial" relationships of intra-abdominal organs. I wish I could give students some of the fifty years of experience I have garnered. We have to work with doctors and nurses both male and female from the emergency room, hospital, and clinics. I have been here in Florida for the past eleven years and will not get into details because everyone would think I was talking about them. Common sense is not very common. The stories and secrets are much the same.

We have enjoyed our nondenominational Pentecostal church and we have many close friends there. I have Bible study every Thursday evening at the Methodist Church and enjoy it thoroughly. I still do my "thing" in real estate and own several commercial and rental properties. I drive a pickup truck as always. I am on the board of our church school and the board of our Hospital Foundation. I don't ever plan on retiring.

Number one eventually came back in the lives of my children approximately ten years ago. She lives in Cleveland, Tennessee, where my three oldest children now live. She has even made a claim that I should buy her a house due to the fact that we had difficulties when we were married. I have refused to do this. But she did persuade my two oldest sons to help her with her mortgage.

Number two has never reentered my life, thank God. I thought I understood the depth of her evilness and mental instability until my youngest son passed away at age thirty-eight. She surpassed even my wildest dreams. He lived most of his adult life in New York City. He married and divorced and had little contact with me or number two, his mother. She only recently communicated with him by Facebook. I never knew that he had medical problems. I had visited him once in New York and he called himself the only son of an only son, and we had a strained relationship. It seemed that he always needed money for rent, computers, or just to survive. I learned from a post that number two placed on Facebook that she knew that he had passed away three months earlier with hemachromatosis (a widespread type of iron storage disease. It causes the body to store dangerously high levels which then become like a poison). It was a shock to his brothers and sisters. It's unbelievable that someone hates so much that even the death of a son is not relayed to his father. That's unadulterated evil and hate, in my opinion. I have asked for God's forgiveness for my feelings concerning number two but unlike him, I don't think I can ever forget.

Summary

My father used to say, "Don't bring me a problem unless you have a solution." I believe some of the solutions to our problems lie in the following:

Poverty

"Cleanliness is next to godliness" is a phrase used first by John Wesley in 1778. As I grew up, this was transliterated to "Poverty is next to godliness." Poverty and Godliness became the same. If you were wealthy you were evil, and if you were poor you were Godly. Wealth and poverty are a thinking problem and are really totally different. My thoughts have slowly evolved. Someone has to pay for the lights, water, and AC/heat to keep a church functioning. Studies show that less than three percent of Christians tithe, or give ten percent of their income, as the Lord commands, to their local church. People argue about whether you should tithe on your gross or adjusted income. I believe God will reward us with either gross or adjusted blessings. In general poverty is still associated with "religiousness," small towns, and rules. I believe both poverty and wealth are a state of mind and a heart matter. Many times I still hear that "Money is the root of all evil." However, First Timothy 6:10 states, "For the love of money is the root of all evil." There is a major difference. Matthew 6:24 states, "No man can serve two masters: For either he will hate the one, and love the other; or else he will hold on to the one, and despise the other. He cannot serve God and mammon (money)." Love makes the difference clear.

I don't remember receiving many gifts from my early childhood, including Christmas. Most Christmases included good food, great desserts, occasionally with family members present, and my mother always having a decorated Christmas tree. The best gifts I received were always books.

Proverbs 23: 7 states, "For as a man thinketh in his heart, so is he." Our thoughts and dreams make us who we are and who we will be. This is summed up in a small thirty-one-page book called *As a Man Thinketh* by James Allen. It was written in 1903 but is easily readable. *Think and Grow Rich* by Napoleon Hill was written in 1937. He gives examples of successful men, how to follow their advice, and ideas of his own about master mind groups and succeeding. *Priests and Kings*, a short book by David High written in 1993 helps show that while only a few people are priests, many are kings who work to bring in funds to pay for the church's and priest's needs. One of my favorite books is *How to Manage Your Money* by Larry Burkett. It is a classic and only one hundred sixty-two pages in length.

Solution

Read the books and put them in action. Find a mentor. Start a business. My ten year old grandson has. Tithe and give offerings.

Education

I believe you must at least finish high school. A diploma is required for most jobs today. You must learn the basics: how to read, write, and use basic math as it was taught in the country schools I attended. I learned that a trade school or college is a necessary decision. Some may need neither. Find out where the library is and use it. Most people use their iPhone for information and are absolutely sure that everything they read on the web is true. Just ask them. I took courses like Greek and Latin etymology, which were and still are extremely useful, and English literature and psychology which I thoroughly enjoyed. I'm thankful my father made a lot of educational decisions for me. My rural upbringing taught me that no matter which decisions are made, we all need to work.

How many books have you read? How long does it take you to read a 300-page book, or have you finished a book you didn't want to read? Did you ever read a book where you didn't understand everything you read or were asked to do something that was hard to do? Have you ever read *The Count of Monte Cristo* (544 pages), *War and Peace* (1296 pages), *All Quiet on the Western Front* (2054 pages), the Bible (1152 pages)? One of these contains history, beautiful stories, poetry, family intrigue, sex, incest, forgiveness. Read it straight through; don't just read the ending or just read the good parts. One study shows that over thirty percent of people never read a book after high school, over forty percent never read a book after college, over fifty-seven percent have started a book but never finished it, and over eighty percent of families have never bought a book or even been in a bookstore in the past five years. Wonder why?

I've read the entire Bible every year in many different translations over the past forty years. Each time is a new and exciting experience. Just look at the lineage of Jesus Christ. It goes through an emigrant, Ruth; a prostitute, Rahab; an adulterer and murderer, David. There are so many translations now that there is no excuse for having to read King James' language. *The Living Bible* is a simple and beautiful paraphrase. *The Message* uses contemporary and understandable English.

Solution

Go to school. Learn the basics—reading, writing, math, and English. Get a job while you're going to school. Not loans!

Abortion

I believe life begins at conception. I have never done an abortion in my life and would never do so even if I were asked. In fact why would anyone ever ask you to perform a procedure or service of any kind if you didn't want to do it or even believe in it?

One study shows that whites make up 61.3 percent of the population, have 37 percent of the total abortions done, and their abortion ratio is 121 abortions per 1000 live births. Hispanics make up 17.8 percent of the population, have 19 percent of the total abortions, and their abortion ratio is 178 abortions per 1000 live births. Blacks make up 13.3 percent of the population (they made up 10.5 percent of the population when I graduated from high school in 1960), have 36 percent of the total abortions done, and their abortion ratio is 420 per 1000 live births. Abortion is racist! Women of color are five times more likely to terminate their pregnancies. Alveda King, niece of Dr. Martin Luther King, Jr., agrees that abortion is racist and says, "Every aborted baby is like a slave in the womb of his or her mother." Maybe Margaret Sanger, when she opened a birth control clinic in 1916 in Brooklyn, had something else in mind.

Solution

Don't murder a child. Take responsibility and keep your child or let him or her be adopted.

Homosexuality

In the Army I treated a young homosexual with venereal warts. When others found out I would not report them, I got an additional ten patients with similar conditions. I treated all with respect as I do all patients and educated them with medical facts. Some of my best friends have been in the LGBTQ classification. Ghandi said, "We should love the sinner and not the sin." The Bible expands this concept. I can love the thief but hate thievery. I can love the liar but hate the lie. I can love the glutton but hate the excessive indulgences and associated medical problems it brings. I can love the alcoholic but hate alcoholism. I can love the drug addict but hate his addiction to opioids and other drugs. I can hate homosexuality but love the homosexual. I can hate adultery but love the adulterer. By the way, I believe that homosexuality is not a genetic problem just as adultery is not a genetic problem. I disagree politically with many people but still love them.

Solution

Love and accept the sinner, not the sin.

Women's Rights

If a woman is in control of her body and can decide when to have an abortion, then why can't she have a hysterectomy when she wants to? In medical school we were taught that the uterus was only good for having babies, bleeding, and getting cancer. Crude but true. If a woman desires a hysterectomy or to have her tubes tied, the government has decided that she must wait thirty days. The insurance companies agree that it is a sterilization procedure and even with pathology present, a woman must wait because she may change her mind. It's easier and much quicker to get an abortion than it is for a woman to have a hysterectomy or her tubes tied.

Why can't a woman be a prostitute if she wants? Prostitution is legal in only one state, Nevada, but not in the entire state. It is only legal in the eight counties that have brothels. Sometimes we can become so tolerant that we accept anything. Matthew 23:24 states, "You blind guides! You strain out a gnat but swallow a camel." Like the country song says, "If you don't stand for something, you'll fall for anything."

Solution

You can't change your sex, gender, or ethnicity. Make the best with what you have and what you are.

Drugs

We had a greater problem with drugs between 1968 and 1972 than we do now because the drugs were illegal then and now are "legally" prescribed opioids. I first recognized the drug problem in 1972 when I entered the Army. It was required that we work in the emergency room on a regular rotation while being on call for surgery. If a patient came in complaining of pain, we gave them a red APC tablet which consisted of aspirin, phenacetin, and caffeine. If the patient returned and said, "Those red tablets don't help the pain," we switched him to a green APC tablet, knowing that just the color change many times gave pain relief.

I believe the real drug problem started ten to twelve years ago when the government decided that pain would become the fifth vital sign. The other four vital signs consisting of blood pressure, pulse, respiration, temperature are all objective findings. Knowing that pain is subjective and perception varies from person to person, it is obvious that there are real problems. We asked patients to rate their pain on a scale of 0–10. The government mandated that we relieve the patient's pain and even had hospitals rated on how the pain was relieved. Ratings were placed on the Internet so everyone could see. In my opinion, there are patients who will overdose and say to their dying breath that they are still in pain. Of course we are taught that our patients always tell the truth. I would never have been convicted in 2015 for the amount of medicine given to the patient that I treated in 1985 who was dying of cancer.

Today it seems we have a problem with prescription opiate addiction. Everything is cyclical and "for everything there is a season" Ecclesiastes 3:1 through 8.

Solution

All addicts have a hole inside that only Jesus Christ can fill. Faith-based programs have the best results and least recidivism.

Race

Color is only a couple of millimeters thick or the same thickness as our skin. Our liver, fat, intestines, muscles, blood, bone, and all the other tissues beneath our skin are all the same color.

Simple? For me it is, but I believe KISS stands for *Keep It Simple for Surgeons.*

Solution

God-given lives have no color!

Codependency

Can we be knights in shining armor or can we be everything to everybody? We are taught now that if you are, then you must handle the guilt and shame which will make you sick both physically and psychologically and can kill you. Thank God that He purposefully forgives and forgets. My treatment for codependency was useful because I became board-certified in addiction medicine as well as general surgery.

Solution

Be the very best of whatever you decide to become. Help and encourage others.

Family

Sociologists Paula Fornby and Andrew Cherlin stated, "A growing body of literature suggests that children who experience multiple transitions in family structure may fair worse developmentally than children raised in stable two-parent families and perhaps even than children raised in stable, single-parent families." The key word in that statement is "stable." You know any unstable families?

I think many of the problems that we have in society now is because of the absence of fathers.

The government cannot be our father. In an article "Adolescent Elephants Need a 'father figure' to Learn From" by Katharine Fielding, she relates the findings and observations of a three-year study by Kate Evans and Stephen Harris. "Like in humans, the 'teenage' years for elephants are characterized by increased risk taking, increased playfulness, and sometimes aggressiveness and a strong desire to explore. And like humans, having a strong 'father figure' to learn from can help ease the transition into adulthood." This concept is included in an article by Wade Horn PhD, "Of Elephants and Men."

One solution was taken away when the Army no longer had a "draft" as it did when I was eighteen years of age. I believe that it is necessary for a young man to have someone besides his father tell him what to do and expect him to do it. There is no asking why, but only that he must do it. I consider it an awesome responsibility to be a father. In my opinion the government can't be a father. I believe that first and foremost we must have God-fearing Christian fathers. Being a father is not based on impregnating women but taking the responsibility for a family, holding them together, and giving wise instruction.

Solution

Be Godly fathers, marry, and take care of your families responsibly. Reinstitute the draft.

Faith

There are some basic truths. We don't all serve the same God! In John 14:6 in an *Amplified Bible*, Jesus answered, "I am the way, the truth, and life, and no man comes to the Father but by me, except through me, except by means of me." No other religion claims that fact. John 8:32 states "You shall know the truth, and the truth shall make you free." Hebrews 11:1 states, "Now faith is the substance of things hoped for, the evidence of things not seen." I believe this!

Solution

Find and become a member of a Bible-believing church.

Secrets

I liken secrets to an anaerobic abscess in the depths of the abdominal cavity. Antibiotics have a difficult time penetrating the abscess and improving the situation. When an abscess is opened, it causes pain. But when the abscess and the anaerobic organisms causing it are exposed to air, the oxygen kills the bacteria. Healing begins! We embolden our secrets by keeping them hidden. God can forgive just as we can but He goes a step further: He performs one of the greatest acts of Grace—He chooses not to remember. We have difficulty in doing that.

Solution

With God's help you can open and drain your abscesses.

Sometimes I had a difficult time separating my earthly father from God, my heavenly Father. Dad didn't believe in coincidences, only miracles. Dad didn't take a vacation. There are no Hebrew words for coincidence or vacation. I used to quote Mark 8:36 to my father, "For what shall it profit a man, if he shall gain the whole world, and lose his own soul?" I always changed that last part to "and lose his own son." I was wrong, my father was right. Maybe that's okay.

Hillbilly Elegy and this book can be depressing. But there is hope in Jesus Christ. Romans 8:28 states, "And we know that all things work together for good to them that love God, to them who are the called according to his purpose." Jeremiah 17:9 in the *Amplified Version* states, "The heart is deceitful above all things and it is extremely sick. Who can understand fully and know its secret motives?"

Dad always said that making decisions was not hard, but sticking to a decision was. He also taught me that all decisions have consequences. No one wants to believe that. Even making no decision is a decision. I believe God doesn't steer parked cars. We must always be moving forward. Faith makes the difference and give us all, hillbillies and country boys, a way out.

ACKNOWLEDGMENTS

All of the aforementioned stories are my own recollections. I know that perception is reality for all my family and friends. As it is for me. If I have knowingly or unknowingly done anything to abuse, intimidate, or harm anyone, in any manner, or in their perception, I ask forgiveness.